PENGUIN BOOKS

1001 WAYS TO SAVE THE PLANET

Bernadette Vallely is the Director of the Women's Environmental Network and has been working on environmental issues for over five years. She has worked at Friends of the Earth and at The Anti-Apartheid Movement and has been involved with Greenpeace, SERA and many other similar organizations.

In early 1988 she co-founded the Women's Environmental Network, which has since grown into an exciting and powerful organization. She is author of *Fundraising is Fun: A Guide for Local Groups* and co-author of *The Sanitary Protection Scandal* and *The Young Person's Guide to Saving the Planet*.

Bernadette Vallely is twenty-eight and lives with her partner, also an environmentalist, in London.

1001 Ways to Save the Planet

Bernadette Vallely

with cartoons by Angela Martin

Penguin Books

PENGUIN BOOKS

Published by the Penguin Group
27 Wrights Lane, London W8 5TZ, England
Viking Penguin Inc., 40 West 23rd Street, New York, New York 10010, USA
Penguin Books Australia Ltd, Ringwood, Victoria, Australia
Penguin Books Canada Ltd, 2801 John Street, Markham, Ontario, Canada L3R 1B4
Penguin Books (NZ) Ltd, 182–190 Wairau Road, Auckland 10, New Zealand

Penguin Books Ltd, Registered Offices: Harmondsworth, Middlesex, England

First published 1990
10 9 8 7 6 5 4 3 2 1

Made and printed on recycled paper in Great Britain by
Richard Clay Ltd, Bungay, Suffolk
Filmset in 11/13½pt Bembo Monophoto

For Althea Joanne

Contents

Introduction

The growing damage to the planet isn't being caused by someone 'out there'. It is fundamentally related to us – the way we live and the things we consume. That simple fact – and the need to accept our responsibility – will be crucial in the fight to save the planet.

It is heartening today to see so many people ready to take positive action for the environment. Opinion polls suggest that more than 50 per cent of us are willing to buy environmentally friendly products even if they cost more. A large majority of motorists would stop using their cars for commuting if alternatives were available.

A smaller percentage of us are willing and able to pay higher prices for organic foods, and as their prices fall, more of us will buy them to stop the over-use of pesticides. We are willing to buy unbleached, recycled paper to save trees and to stop the pollution of our river systems. We have foregone aerosols for containers that are less damaging to the environment.

Many people are now asking what they can do apart from being green consumers and switching soap-powder brands. Information is the key to making the right choices for other aspects of our lives. *1001 Ways to Save the Planet* will provide you with that information. No one can do everything at once, but this book will give you ideas. Do things you feel comfortable with at first. Take one step at a time. If we all did just a small percentage of the things listed in this book, we would go a long way towards solving some of our most pressing ecological problems.

Each of the 1001 things to do listed here is short, and most of them are simple. They may stimulate you to get in touch with a group or organization or to read other books, but in the main they represent straightforward actions that most people can take.

They may save you money.

They may encourage you to stop doing something you always suspected was wrong or wasteful.

They may change your lifestyle.

They may all add up to your becoming a conscious, aware person, ready to SAVE THE PLANET!

Sometimes I can't see the trees for the wood.

Acknowledgements

I am indebted to Charo Lamas, who has helped me type and retype the manuscript with joy and inspiring competence, and to Sandra van der Feen for spending time on the telephone to check facts and figures on my behalf.

Thanks must also be given to those who have supported me with love and enthusiasm and who have read and commented on the manuscript, suggesting their own ways to save the planet, supplying me with statistics and references, information and ideas, and educating me on many environmental issues that I knew little about: Sue Adams, Stewart Boyle, Dave Buffin of the Pesticides Trust, Miranda Castro of the Spectrum Clinic, Liz Cook, Alison Costello, Guy Dauncey, Pat Fleming of Friends of the Earth US, Ann Link, Jan McHarry, Brigitte Mierau, Jose Pepper, Debbie Silver, Hugh Singh of Plantlife, Tessa Strickland of Penguin Books and my mother, Susan Vallely.

Acknowledgements are due to the hundreds of organizations and individuals who have helped me to prepare this book, from those who supplied literature and information sheets to those who helped me dig deep to find answers that might not otherwise have surfaced. Readers of this book should be aware of the dedication, professionalism and sheer stamina that make up just some of the qualities of those who work in the environmental world. They include: Animal Aid; Stuart Bell, Pension Investment Research Consultants; Michael Birkin; Liz Bisset, Islington Borough Council; Mary

Blake, Friends of the Earth UK; Anne Brant, Balloons &
Clowns Ltd, USA; Hartwin Busch; John Button; Giles
Chitty, Barchester Green Investors; Karen Christensen; the
Civic Trust; Madeline Cobbing, Greenpeace UK; Sue Coffin,
National Magazine Company; the Conservation Foundation;
Keith Corbett, the Herpetological Conservation Trust; the
Council for the Protection of Rural England; Simon Counsell
and Adrian Davies, Friends of the Earth UK; Nigel Dudley;
Energy Efficiency Office; Environment Defense Fund, USA;
James Erlichman; Kharis Fausset, Friends of the Earth UK;
Ferguson's Building, N. Ireland; Herbert Girardet; David
Goldbeck; Pad Green, Friends of the Earth UK; the Green-
house Crisis Foundation, USA; the *Green Magazine*; the
Haldane Trust; Tony Hare, Plantlife; Jonathon Hopkins; Liz
Howlett; Johnson Wax; Briony Jones; Julia Langer, Friends of
the Earth Canada; the London Food Commission; Debra
Lynn-Dadd; LYNX; Robin Maynard, Friends of the Earth
UK; Kai Millaird, Friends of the Earth Canada; Fiona Murie,
London Hazards Centre; Natural Resources Defense Council,
USA; David Newick, Greencard BCC Card Centre; Andy
Ottoman, Greenpeace UK; Pauline Pears, the Henry Double-
day Research Association; Gord Perks, Greenpeace Canada;
Colin Redman, National Deaf Children's Society; James
Richardson, Anti-Apartheid Movement; Royal Society for
Nature Conservation; Royal Society for the Prevention of
Cruelty to Animals; Carole Rubin, Canadian Environmental
Network; Anne Scott, Royal Society for the Protection of
Birds; Seventh Generation Trading, USA; Catriona Slovach,
Pension Investment Research Consultants; Michelle Sweet,
Pollution Probe Canada; Alistair Townley, GreenGauge;
United Nations Environment Programme; the Vegan Society;
the Vegetarian Society; Joan Walley, MP; Clive Williams,
Faculty of Environmental Urban Spaces, Polytechnic of
North London; World Wide Fund for Nature.

Particular thanks go to the organization Common Ground, whose work I find inspiring, poetic and unique and to whom I owe much of the re-affirmation of my own love of the countryside and, especially, the beauty and nobility of trees.

Half of the proceeds from this book will go to the Women's Environmental Network, an independent, non-profit organization committed to educating, informing and empowering women who care about the environment. Women and men are equally welcome to join, and for more information, or if you want to share your own ideas on how to save the planet, please write to the Women's Environmental Network, 287 City Road, London, EC1V ILA. Please include a stamped addressed envelope or £1 if you need a reply.

The Green Home

The Kitchen

Use a 'green' kettle

A kettle is an important part of your kitchen, and you're likely to use it several times each day. To save energy, buy an automatic kettle that can boil as little as one cup, or use a small kettle on your cooker.

Descale your kettle

Descaling your kettle prevents the build-up of fur inside and around the element, which in turn leads to a longer boiling time and wasted energy. You will find that filtered water stops the kettle furring up so quickly. Use descalers that are non-toxic and not tested on animals. These are now relatively easy to find. Try using a strong vinegar solution as a cheap and simple alternative. Rinse the kettle out carefully afterwards.

Use small pans for cooking

Use the smallest pan necessary for cooking food. Don't waste energy on heating up the metal of an oversized saucepan. Turn down the heat to match the size of the pan.

Use steamers and dividers

You don't need three saucepans to cook three different types of vegetable. One good steamer or pan divider will do. You then need only one ring or burner, and steamed vegetables taste far better than boiled ones and are more nutritious.

Use saucepan lids

Put the lids on your saucepans. There are two advantages: lids save energy, as water and food boil more quickly; they also reduce the condensation in your kitchen, which leads to damp. Turn the heat down once water has boiled, saving further energy. Cook with the right amount of water. Most foods need only enough water to cover them.

Stop running the water

Using running water to wash your dishes is extremely costly and wasteful. It is far better to get a bowl or to use a sink plug.

Use cold water

Use cold water for rinsing dishes, washing vegetables and a host of other kitchen tasks. This will save the precious energy it takes to heat the water and will keep your fuel bills low. You could put a note near the taps to remind you.

Ventilate your kitchen

If you are using a gas cooker, you will be saving lots of money on your energy bills because electricity power stations in Britain are so inefficient. But you could be storing up trouble. According to American scientists, young children could be especially at risk from respiratory illnesses resulting from badly ventilated kitchens in which gas is used for cooking. Open the window or use a solar-powered ventilating system.

Clean your tumble dryer

The tumble dryer uses large amounts of energy to keep a drum circulating hot air around with clothes in order to dry them. A small lint screen filters the air that enters the drum. Clean it regularly. A screen with any fluff or wool on it will make the machine work harder, wasting energy.

Service your fridge

Virtually every household has a refrigerator, but most people don't realize that these machines gobble up energy, using valuable resources and contributing to acid rain and global warming. Servicing your fridge can make a major difference to your electricity bills and to the performance of the machine. Check the seal for leaks or loose rubber gaskets; clean the coils at the back of the machine at least once a year; use a thermometer to check the temperature inside the refrigerator; and look out for tell-tale signs like the frost building up too quickly or the walls of the unit 'sweating'. Defrost the machine several times a year, and never let frost build up to more than 5 mm ($\frac{1}{4}$ in). Cover all foods, especially liquids, to keep frost down. Proper attention to your fridge will keep it efficient, save energy and extend its working life.

Design your life to save energy in the fridge

Don't put your fridge near the cooker or other hot appliances. Don't leave the door open longer than necessary and buy only as much food as will fill the shelves with ease, so that air can circulate. Remember to turn the temperature down to save energy in winter. Get advice about the correct temperature. By thinking a little in advance, you could save money on your bills and save energy at the same time. Design yourself an energy-efficient lifestyle.

Dispose of your old fridge carefully

Old fridges can be a hazard. CFCs can leak, and that is when they cause the most damage. These substances are very stable and will last until they reach the ozone layer. Then they break down, releasing chlorine, which destoys the ozone layer. Ask your local authority or the manufacturer to recycle the CFCs safely. Throwing your fridge out could also be a death trap for small children, who could get caught inside and suffocate. Insist that the machine is disposed of with consideration to the environment.

Buy a CFC-reduced, energy-efficient fridge and freezer

If you are about to go out and purchase a new fridge or freezer, there are two major considerations.

First, it must be energy–efficient. In the USA refrigeration accounts for 7 per cent of the total electricity used and one third of the average household energy bill. Check for new energy-saving features. Most companies now produce at least one model. The Consumers' Association gives details of running costs. The difference in your electricity bill between the best and worst models can be up to £30 for fridges and £100 a year for freezers. For the environment it can mean a great deal more.

Secondly, your fridge or freezer must not threaten the ozone layer. Buy a model that is equipped with fewer CFCs in the insulating foam.

Check your halon fire extinguisher

Forty per cent of all household accidents happen in the kitchen, and a great many of these are fires. Fire experts in the United States suggest that 16 per cent of fatal fires begin in the kitchen, and at least 300,000 such fires are thought to occur every year. Although a fire extinguisher is an important part of your safety equipment, halon fire extinguishers are known to be serious ozone depletors. It is obvious that we have to be alert to the dangers of fires in the home, but for electric, grease and liquid fires (like hot fats) buy a halon-free extinguisher or a good fire blanket that will deprive a fire of oxygen. Do learn how to treat fires responsibly, and teach other members of your household too.

Change your boiler

Over half the fuel bill in an average home is generated by

heating the house and the water. A well-maintained gas central-heating system uses less energy and produces less pollution than either an electric or a solid-fuel system. The most efficient type of boiler available is the gas condensing boiler, which extracts heat from the waste flue gases because it allows them to condense in the boiler. These boilers cost more, but if your current model is old, or if you are moving to a new home, the investment could save you 10 to 15 per cent of your fuel bills. Modern controls and regular annual maintenance of your boiler could save you as much as 20 per cent of the bills.

Get rid of cockroaches safely

Cockroaches are nasty insects to find at home or in your workplace. They make holes in piles of packaging or near pipes and breed very quickly. Traditionally they have been sprayed with pesticides, but there are more acceptable and surer methods of getting rid of these disease-carrying insects. (Their eggs are protected in capsules, so they can often survive pesticide spraying anyway.) Gaps of more than 5 mm ($\frac{1}{4}$ in) need to be cemented, but the most obvious expedients are to keep your house clean and to check under and behind surfaces, especially behind fridges. To kill cockroaches use a mixture of flour, plaster of paris, powdered sugar and borax or bicarbonate of soda, which cockroaches will eat. They also seem to be attracted to sweets, so glass jars containing sweets could trap them.

Recycle bottles

We use 6 billion glass bottles every year in Britain, 5 billion of which are thrown straight into dustbins. The other 1 billion includes beer bottles, which are recycled many times, and milk bottles, which are used an average of twenty-four times before being crushed and melted into glass again. By recycling you save oil — each tonne of waste glass uses 136 litres (30 gallons) less oil than new glass — and therefore precious resources. Use bottle banks.

Use recycled glass

Light-green glass for drinking glasses, jugs and kitchenware, made by cooperatives in Spain, gives you the perfect recycled product. It is slightly thicker than normal glass and is tough and hardwearing.

Insulate your dishwasher

There are no standards that regulate the insulation of dishwashers, which means they can be inefficient, especially smaller models without even basic coverings. This is especially true in cold climates or when a dishwasher is installed against an outside wall, as the temperature outside may affect the water temperature. If you can't buy a model with thick insulation, then consider boxing it in yourself. The tiny cost will be quickly recouped through greater efficiency, and you will also have a quieter machine.

Use your dishwasher the greenest way

It is arguable that using dishwashers can never be green. They use less water — about 20 litres (4¼ gallons) a day versus the 40–60 litres used when washing dishes by hand for a family of four — and less energy (1.5 kWh versus an average of 2–3 kWh), but when the energy needed to manufacture the machines is taken into account, there is little saving. What is clear, however, is that dishwashers save time and labour. You can make sure that your dishwasher is as green as possible by making sure you always have a full load, selecting a temperature at least 10 °C (50 °F) lower than recommended, washing large dishes by hand and using a cold-fill option to save energy.

Plan small meals carefully

If you live on your own or often have to cook for yourself, you may find that a multi-cooker or slow cooker, which uses as little electricity as a light bulb, could save you money and energy. You may choose to cook a large amount and freeze or store some for another meal later on. This will also save energy.

Don't use a microwave

There is a widely held belief that a microwave can save you energy, but a recent study by the Canadian Government shows that you save a grand total of $10 (about £5) a year in electricity costs if you use a microwave rather than an electric stove. Only 35–40 per cent of the energy microwaves use is actually used to cook the food; the rest is wasted. A recent study in the British medical journal the *Lancet* found that microwave cooking of milk, cheese, meat and fish creates potentially dangerous abnormal aminoacids that are neuro-toxic, which means that they may kill brain and nerve cells and are toxic to the liver and kidneys. A British Government report in 1989 found that one third of the ovens tested failed to heat food uniformly to a temperature that will kill bacteria or listeria. As microwaves are intended primarily for pre-processed foods, the health-conscious greenie will do well to avoid them.

Beware of the pretty dish

Glazed pottery dishes, fruit bowls and food containers may contain lead and cadmium. Concern has been raised in Europe about the continued use of toxic metals in glazes used by potters who make their own pots and in those that come from developing countries. Once again there is a double problem – the lead and cadmium are harmful to the environment but also potentially harmful to us through our food. Buying industrial pottery from sources you can trust is usually a good bet because the glazes will have been sealed.

Open the windows

Instead of using artificially created air fresheners from aerosol cans, try a greener alternative. Use potpourri mixes of herbs and dried flower petals for a natural smell. Most air fresheners in aerosol cans use chemicals like limonene and imidazoline, which work by blocking the sense of smell and giving off a pungent odour that masks everything else. They are suspected carcinogens in animals. Aerosol companies may have removed the CFCs, but they use hydrocarbons that are 'soft' greenhouse gases instead. Hydrocarbons also contribute to local smog. Aerosols are not biodegradable and take more energy to produce than they are worth. If you cannot easily find potpourri, try opening a window!

Use food containers

Instead of wrapping everything in cling wrap, aluminium foil and paper, get some good sturdy food containers and save on waste. Save energy in your fridge by covering food with a lid.

Don't throw your waste down the sink

Sink waste-disposal units are energy-intensive and encourage bad housekeeping. Save your food scraps for the compost heap instead of adding to our polluted waste systems.

Washing up your dishes

Use the smallest possible bowl in which your dishes will fit.
Save time and energy by steeping them in water first to
loosen difficult stains.

Cadmium-free plastics

Cadmium is an acutely toxic heavy metal, and there is
evidence that even tiny quantities have reproductive effects.
Once taken out of the ground, concentrated and released into
the environment, it stays there for ever. The millions of
kitchen bowls, storage bins, dustbins, brushes and pans that
we buy each year are made from plastics that may contain
cadmium; bright-red and orange plastics are the main candi-
dates. Because of pressure from the European Community the
production of cadmium will be curtailed in coming years.
Some companies have already removed cadmium from their
plastics, and you should look for the cadmium-free label
before you buy.

Store and re-use plastic carrier bags

The first lesson is to learn to say NO to carrier bags, but if
you have them, do not throw them away. Re-use them as
rubbish bags.

Do not use paper towels

We buy 280 million kitchen towels every year in Britain, and
billions in the USA, where even dishcloths and tea towels
have been replaced by the paper throwaway. The paper
comes from trees and is bleached using chlorine, unless the
labels say otherwise, which means the pollution, in the form
of dioxins and furans, of our waterways. Use clean cloths to

wipe up spills, and rinse them frequently. Do not be fooled by advertising that tells you that a cloth is unhygienic.

Get good lighting

If you have a big kitchen, you are likely to spend quite a lot of time in it, and you will want to fit the best lights for the environment. Energy-efficient lighting produces up to 75 per cent less carbon dioxide, the main greenhouse gas, than ordinary bulbs. Good lights for the kitchen will be more expensive initially, but within a year you will be saving money.

Look after your kitchen

Kitchen utensils should be kept clean and in good condition. Cheap or badly made utensils just won't last and will cost you more in the long run. Catering shops are a good place to find well-made utensils.

Find ecological washing-up liquid

Washing up liquids are generally made from petrochemical-based derivatives. Waterways around the world have been polluted and destroyed by oil slicks and secondary pollution from the petrochemical industry. Avoid fragrant and coloured washing liquids; they have usually been tested on animals. Campaign for your favourite brand to label its ingredients clearly. Use brands whose labels declare them to be cruelty-free and to contain ingredients that you can trust.

Use a pressure cooker

Save energy when cooking: use a pressure cooker for vegetables, stews and tasty, quick meals.

Make jams and chutneys

A friend of mine is trying to campaign for a two-week public holiday in early September so that everyone can help pick fresh fruit and vegetables and begin pickling, making jams and chutneys and preserving in syrup. Mrs Beaton wrote in 1859, 'To be acquainted with the periods when things are in season is one of the most essential pieces of knowledge which enter into the art of cookery.' Her recipes include apple jam, damson cheese and quince jelly. Fruits in season are certainly much cheaper, and by making our own preserves we can save money, use up the jam jars we have been collecting and produce a really wonderful alternative to sugar-laden jams from the supermarket.

Get rid of useless gadgets

Some gadgets that are foisted upon us at birthdays, Christmas and weddings use up energy and waste resources. Do not buy them if you have a choice, and think carefully about their usefulness. Surprisingly, the coffee percolator and electric frying pan come out badly in terms of energy use, and the waste compactor, waffle iron and electric toaster are not far behind. An electric blender uses very little energy and costs a few pence to operate, so it could make a worthwhile utensil. Forget electric carving knives and specialist egg pans unless you are cooking for a restaurant.

Compost your kitchen waste

Collect the organic matter that you throw away each week in a bucket or tub and compost it in your garden or patio for a rich fertilizer. Feed scraps to pets, and save some for the birds too.

Switch to gas

Natural gas is over 40 per cent more energy-efficient than electric heating or cooking. It makes economic sense to switch to a better fuel.

Wrap up without aluminium

Aluminium foil comes from mined bauxite, some of which is derived from destroyed rainforest areas. It is extremely energy-intensive to produce, using nearly 6 tonnes of oil for every tonne of aluminium. Re-use tubs and pots for storing food, and use dish covers made from glass for the oven.

Check your pots and pans

Aluminium was first used for cooking by the French nobility of the early 1800s, but as the price fell, it soon lost its glamour and everyone was able to cook with the wonderful new metal. An increase in aluminium in the body has been linked to diseases such as Alzheimer's disease. Many people feel that as the aluminium in pots and pans has a chemical reaction, especially when acidic foods like tomatoes and rhubarb are cooked, we should avoid them and opt for stainless steel, cast-iron and enamelled cookware. Don't use aluminium tea-pots either, as tea itself is said to contain high levels of aluminium.

Pack your freezer

You can save energy and help your freezer to run better if it's filled to capacity. Buy foods that are cheaper in bulk, and make several dishes together in the oven to save energy and money.

Green up your kitchen units

Chipboard is still used for many of the world's kitchen units these days. The wood is chipped, then stuck back together in long sheets with formaldehyde. About one in five people are thought to be sensitive to formaldehyde, and the gas seeps from chipboard products for many years. Do not buy tropical hardwood either. Go for a locally produced hardwood if you can afford it, second-hand units or a soft wood (such as pine) from a sustainable source.

Use recycled black plastic bags

Every year we spend billions of pounds on black plastic refuse bags to collect the rubbish and waste that we have accumulated. Ninety-six per cent of our rubbish is technically recyclable, and if we recycled as much as we could, there would be less need for black bags. Until that happens, we will continue to use them, so at least try to buy rubbish sacks made from recycled plastic.

Separate your waste

All over Britain, Canada and the USA we are waking up to the fact that we consume and waste precious resources. The average household throws away over 2 tonnes of rubbish each year, creating a mountain of stinking, rusting, chemical-filled garbage. A large proportion of it could be recycled. About 30 per cent of our rubbish is paper and card, easily recycled; another 10 per cent is glass, with excellent recycling potential; another 30 per cent is organic, which can be composted. The rest is plastics, metals and packaging made from two or more types of material, for which recycling is difficult, if not impossible. On average 4 per cent of the waste is babies' disposable nappies. By learning to separate your waste in the kitchen you will start to create the climate for successful recycling programmes, and you can already do a lot without formal programmes. The main point is to be conscious of the waste that you put into the dustbin and to think of the effect that its short life has had on the environment.

Rainforest-free kitchenware

Half a hectare (1 acre) of tropical rainforest is destroyed every second. The forests represent the richest source of life on earth, maintaining half of all living creatures. One of the ways in which we destroy the rainforest is by demanding millions of kitchen bowls, knife handles, breadbins and chopping boards each year. If you buy these items, always check where the wood has come from. A hardwood is more likely than not to have come from a forest, so avoid the product if you are not sure. Small companies are now emerging that produce goods made from the wood of sustainably forested trees. These are more environmentally friendly.

Disinfect without harm

When I grew up I used to think that disinfectant came from hospitals and was a type of medicinal cleaner. I never thought that it could be poisonous or toxic, and yet today's disinfectants contain a number of volatile chemicals like trichlorophenol, cresol, benzalkonium chloride and formaldehyde. Far better to use borax and hot water and simply to keep your household as clean as possible. One American hospital monitored bacteria for a year while using borax and found that it completely satisfied all its germicidal requirements and cost less too.

Use vinegar to clean glass and mirrors

Save yourself money: use vinegar, water and paper for a sharp cleaner that is better value than the heavily marketed aerosol sprays that release tiny drops of irritating ammonia. You may have to rub hard at first to get rid of the build-up of the old cleaner, so be prepared for a second clean.

Always use the minimum

Whether you are washing or cleaning clothes, surfaces or dishes, a good environmental rule is to use the absolute minimum to get the job done. We often apply cleaners so liberally that most of the product goes down the sink or drain. Save energy, avoid pollution and always use the minimum.

Use lemon juice

Lemon juice can be used as a mild bleach, for cleaning metals and copper and for descaling. You do not have to buy bottles of lemon juice; the lemon itself comes in its own biodegradable packaging! Save the rind to put around your roses to ward off cats.

Clean your oven without having to use aerosols

Use a paste of baking soda and water for a non-toxic alternative to sodium hydroxide- and hydrocarbon-filled aerosols when you clean your oven. A container filled with a pump-action spray and filled with washing-up liquid (green, of course) and borax in warm water is a good alternative cleaner.

Try your own dishwasher soap

If you are dissatisfied with the dishwasher powders that you are offered, particularly because they contain strong chemicals and are mostly tested on animals, try making your own. For a fairly good alternative, use borax from a chemist or hardware store, mixed with half as much baking soda.

Get rid of tea stains with baking soda

Use the cheapest of all scouring powders, baking soda, to get rid of tea and coffee stains in cups and on surfaces. Ninety-five per cent of the average powder cleaner is chalk, with added perfumes, bleaches and detergent. Chlorinated powdered bleaches produce fumes when wet and can be irritating to the eyes, nose and throat. As well as baking soda, you can use borax or even table salt as a good abrasive.

Use a water filter

Clean, safe water should be on tap for everyone, but persistent use of nitrates and pesticides, combined with neglect by the water industry, has resulted in higher and higher levels of bacteria, heavy metals, lead and aluminium in tap water. Vital for the lives of billions of people and animals across the world, we have to campaign for it not to be polluted, over-used up and wasted. Buy a water filter if you can afford it, but everyone should demand cleaner water.

Grow spider plants

The spider plant, or *Chlorophytum*, has been a favourite house plant for over two hundred years. It is fast-growing and virtually pest-free. Even those who don't know anything about plant care can usually manage to grow a spider plant, which needs lots of water in spring and summer and very little in winter. Recently, however, it has been discovered that *Chlorophytum* can absorb formaldehyde vapours, making it a 'pollution absorber'. You might consider growing spider

plants if you have allergies and think you are susceptible to
formaldehyde.

Return all returnable bottles

Some of the bottles you buy are returnable, and you often get
a few pence for them. An efficient system operates in bars and
pubs for the collection of beer bottles, for example. But you
can also return some medicine bottles to pharmacies and soft
drink bottles to local shops. Don't leave empty bottles to
gather dust: why not spend an hour returning them on your
next day off?

Buy hardwearing rubber gloves

Don't waste resources by buying throw-away gloves. Thicker
and more hardwearing ones will last far longer, although you
may have to look in a hardware shop for them. Good
gardening gloves are essential too and should last for years.

Use cloth napkins

Paper napkins are a wasteful and expensive use of trees and
energy. Cloth napkins have been around for centuries: choose
them as a washable and reusable alternative. Paper napkins are
generally bleached with chlorine, adding to pollution in the
place where they are made, and the use of trees for such a
disposable product is questionable. If you travel, get into the
habit of taking your own napkin with you.

Save aluminium

Save ring pulls from cans, milk bottle tops and clean aluminium foil for collection by local charities that sell it for recycling.

Use old tea for your plants

Feed your plants with left-over tea from the pot. I've fed mine with tea for years, and they love it. (Don't use milk or coffee, though.) You can also put tea leaves on the compost heap.

Keep your kitchen clean

One way to ensure that you are not visited by mice, rats and infestations of insects is by keeping your kitchen clean. Cleaning means looking under the refrigerator, cleaning behind the cooker and picking up things when you drop them as well as making sure that you sweep and wash surfaces and floors regularly. I use baking soda on the floors and surfaces and sometimes a little rosemary essential oil for a fresh, sweet smell.

The Bathroom

Cultivate spiders

There are hundreds of thousands of types of spider, and they all seem to end up in your bathtub. But spiders are an important part of the ecosystem. They live and eat all the creepy crawlies you don't like – houseflies, earwigs, cockroaches and other insects that can spread disease. They are, in turn, an important source of food for birds. Most of them are completely harmless and very small. The one in your bathtub is usually the male *Tegenaria gigantea*, looking for a mate. He has fallen into the tub from the ceiling and been trapped. Turning on the water will drown him. In the tropical forests of Brazil, where gigantism is the norm, there is a bird-eating spider, but you'll find it unlikely to come up through your plug hole! Cultivate spiders: don't kill them.

Avoid chemical toilet cleaners

Toilets, as we know them, were invented in Scotland ten thousand years ago. The inhabitants of the Orkney Islands built the first latrine system, a dug-out channel system designed to carry waste from the home to a nearby stream. They were aware of the dangers of their own waste even then. Today we put bleaches, scourers, cleaners, sprays and toilet blocks into our toilets to keep them clean. Natural micro-organisms exist that break down and dispose of human excrement. By using so many chemicals we actually delay that process. Toilet blocks can contain paradichlorobenzene, which is highly toxic if swallowed and is reported to have caused cancers in laboratory animals. It is persistent in the environment. Use vinegar-based toilet cleaners that have not been tested on animals.

Turn off the tap

Dripping taps waste enormous amounts of energy. A fast-dripping hot tap could fill a bath every day. Taps should be repaired if they are faulty, and rubber washers should always be in good condition.

Take a shower

The average bathtub holds 136 litres (30 gallons) of water. The average five-minute shower uses only 68 litres (15 gallons). Over a year, millions of people taking showers instead of baths could save billions of gallons of hot water, which in turn would save energy and reduce pollution and sewage problems.

Share a bath

If you cannot use a shower in your home, you can at least share your bathwater, which would cut the amount of energy needed to heat and produce the bath water by half! This would be as energy-efficient as taking a shower.

Use pure soap

Most dermatologists agree that pure soap and warm water is the best way of cleaning the skin. Fragrances, tonics and other added ingredients can irritate the skin and can even cause allergies; they also, of course, add to the stockpile of synthetic chemicals and manufacturing processes that are polluting our environment. Strong substances remove the skin's layer of protective oils along with the grease and grime.

Scrub your skin with a washcloth

Use a cotton washcloth to remove grit and bacteria without chemicals. You may find it a better alternative to the expensive sea sponges that come from the Mediterranean and strip the sea of its natural marine life.

Make your own talcum powder

Talcum powder bought in a shop may well be contaminated with cancer-causing asbestos fibres. This is because the talc is often mined in the same geological areas as asbestos. You can make your own talc with cornflour, arrowroot or oat flour, and add ground-up herbs or dried flowers for natural fragrances.

Don't throw your sanitary wear down the toilet

Sanitary towels and tampons are labelled 'fully flushable', and the manufacturers maintain that they can be easily flushed away. But throwing them down the toilet is not the last of towels or tampons. In Britain around 50 per cent of our sewage is untreated and so goes out to sea without any treatment at all. That means that literally billions of sanitary towels and tampons are left to float around in the water. They take about 120 days to biodegrade, and the plastic backing strips do not biodegrade at all. They are washed up on beaches and get caught up in fishing nets, and, as they contain bacteria and faecal contamination, they make a pretty bad meal for an inquiring seabird. Wrap yours in paper bags manufactured for the purpose and put them in the dustbin. No other European country allows sanitary wear to be disposed of so casually via the sewerage system.

Don't buy rainforest bathroom fittings

After pine the most popular wooden bathroom fittings come from tropical rainforests. Mahogany, a rich, luxurious wood, is used to make toilet seats, shelving, towel racks, mirror frames and toilet-roll holders. Major department stores around the world promote these fittings, contributing directly to rainforest destruction. When a mahogany tree is felled, up to a hundred others may be cut and burned simply because they are not as valuable financially. Don't buy rainforest fittings. Stick to alternatives like pine or glass.

Go for squeaky-green hair

In Britain we spend over £150 million a year on shampoos, and the market is growing by 10 per cent a year. Most shampoos are made from the same ingredients, mainly synthetic detergents, a bit like washing-up liquids. If you wash your hair, then rinse it, you are likely to wash off the herbs, perfumes, oils and added extras. Hair does not generally need conditioning creams either. Do not buy shampoos that have been tested on animals.

Mix your own hair conditioner

If you need hair conditioner, instead of using synthetically
produced hair conditioners why not mix up your own? Plain
yoghurt mixed with egg and a quarter teaspoon of nutmeg
makes a really wonderful conditioner. No plastic, no chemicals, no additives.

Beware of dandruff shampoos

The British anti-dandruff market is big business and worth
over £50 million per year. To avoid the embarrassment of
dandruff, we allow our scalps to be poisoned with chemicals
like selenium sulfide, cresol, formaldehyde and resorcinol.
Most of these are toxic substances that can easily be absorbed
through the skin, can burn eyelids and can even cause drowsiness and unconsciousness. They are tested on animals and
produced in huge quantities only to be poured down our
sinks into the water system. Professor David George from the
University of Utah in the USA says, 'Dandruff is not a
disease. Most people have it.'

Brush your teeth

Recent studies have shown that high nitrate levels found in
food and water used as fertilizers to grow vegetables and
fruits can be dangerous to your health. In the body nitrates
can form cancer-producing nitrosamines, and the World
Health Organization has recommended that we reduce our
intake. One report suggests that up to 60 per cent of the
nitrates absorbed by our bodies is produced by food bacteria
in the mouth. Regular brushing and flossing of teeth can
reduce the intake.

*

Clean your teeth with cleaner paste

Most toothpastes on the market today contain all kinds of artificial chemicals to keep the dentist away, but they may not be all that good for us. Sugar substitutes such as saccharin are known to cause cancer in animals, yet they are added to toothpaste to give it a sugary taste. Other ingredients may include ethanol, formaldehyde, ammonium, titanium dioxide and artificial flavourings and colourings. Titanium dioxide is used as a whitener in toothpaste. It has led to acidic pollution in river systems, and Greenpeace has been campaigning to end its production completely. Many natural toothpastes, without any of these ingredients, are available from health-food stores and supermarkets.

Turn off the water as you brush your teeth

You don't need to let the water run while you're brushing your teeth. It's just a habit. Get into the greener habit of turning off the tap as you are brushing. If the whole nation did this, we could save many millions of gallons of water.

Forget the electric toothbrush!

We buy 55 million toothbrushes in Britain every year, but only a small percentage of us go as far as buying an electric toothbrush. It does not use a lot of energy, but the batteries are wasteful, needing fifty times as much energy to produce as they provide. They don't really clean teeth any better than ordinary toothbrushes and are a waste of money and re-sources.

Non-toxic shaving cream

Don't use aerosol spray cans of shaving cream if you can help it. They are filled with chemicals that are ozone-depletors or greenhouse gases and are made from synthetic chemicals. Try a cheaper non-toxic alternative with light vegetable oil or plain soap.

Cut out the disposable razor

Believe it or not, according to archaeologists early man shaved himself with sharpened flints and shells as long ago as 20,000 years BC. The throwaway variety didn't appear until much later, in 1903, when King Gillette, a failed door-to-door salesman, hit upon the idea when he was shaving one morning. Every day in the USA, 5 million disposable razors are binned, making them a profitable but wasteful use of energy and raw materials. Use an electric shaver, or grow a beard and cut out the disposable razor.

Keep a tub of baking soda in the bathroom

Don't bother to use scouring powders or creams in the bathroom. Your bath, tiles and sink can be cleaned with baking soda or borax for no extra effort.

Lag your hot-water tank

Although 90 per cent of British homes have a lagged hot-water tank, much lagging is thin and badly fitted. You will find that a thick insulation jacket for your tank will reduce your electricity bills and save energy.

The Living Room

Use extra-thick curtains

If you sew a backing on your curtains to make them extra-thick, you'll find that they will prevent the heat in your living room and bedroom from escaping through the window. Curtain lining is much more cost-effective than double glazing, and floor-to-ceiling curtains keep even the coldest temperatures at bay.

Block up your fireplace

According to US statistics, 8 per cent of the heating of our homes escapes through the chimney. If you're not using your fireplace, it should be blocked up carefully, so long as you don't block all ventilation, which would cause condensation.

Turn off the remote control on your TV

In Britain around 7 million remote-control television sets are thought to be switched off at night by the remote control button alone leaving the TV to use a quarter of its power all night long. This unnecessary and lazy habit helps to generate an extra 200,000 tonnes of carbon dioxide each year, according to Friends of the Earth. It calculates that the wasted energy costs us around £12 million per year.

Watch green TV

The television sets used in Britain create over 7 million tonnes of carbon dioxide, a greenhouse gas, yet we could be using more energy-efficient televisions. If you have to buy a television, ask about the relative electricity consumption. Don't buy those with remote controls.

Recycle magazines

Every year in the UK we buy over 100 million magazines, made from millions of trees. Magazines printed on glossy paper can be difficult to recycle at present, but you could be creative by taking them to your local doctor's surgery, hospital or dentist. Only buy those you really want to read.

Use cornflour or baking soda to clean your rugs and carpets

Powdered carpet cleaners are usually baking soda with added perfume, packaged in an attractive way. Liquid shampoos are potentially more dangerous, as they contain ingredients such chemicals as perchloroethylene, a known human carcinogen, and naphthalene. These are extremely toxic and should be used only as a last resort. Try shaking ordinary baking soda or cornflour over your carpets or cleaning them with a mixture of white vinegar and boiled water for stubborn stains. Ordinary washing-up liquid is good as a shampoo.

Polish your furniture with olive oil

For wooden furniture that has been badly stained, try polishing with olive oil instead of using aerosols with phenols (possible human carcinogens) and nitrobenzenes. Mix the oil with white vinegar and water for varnished woods. Save the ozone layer, reduce global warming and energy consumption and save yourself some money too.

Avoid foam sofas

Polyurethane foam ignites easily and gives off a thick black smoke that contains cyanides. Literally thousands of people have been killed or injured in foam fires, and firefighters and safety officials advise against their use withou protection. The foam itself is known to cause canc mals.

Recycle your telephone

Without a doubt, the telephone is our most important mode of communication. Until fairly recently the British telephone was the property of the telephone company, but now as in many countries around the world, telephones can be purchased in shops in almost every high street. Every year British Telecom recycles about 4.5 million telephones. They are stripped, and the electronic components are re-used. Metals such as gold, silver and palladium are recycled separately, and the 1,700 tonnes of granulated plastics are melted for other uses. Instead of throwing away your telephone, send it back to the manufacturer for recycling.

Go without the phone book

Telephone directories are made from precious paper, yet many of us never need them. Computerized operator systems can give you most numbers cheaply and effectively, and you may find that all you need is the *Yellow Pages* or your local community or business directory. This could cut down on the number of phone books that are given free to households every year. Apparently the glue used on the spines of telephones directories make them harder to recycle. You may like to take that up with the telephone company.

Go for negative ions

Negative ions are really positive. They can make all the difference to the atmosphere in a room. Many people use air ionizers to improve the amount of useful negative ions in the room, especially if they suffer from asthma, hayfever, bronchitis or migraine. A negative voltage refreshes a room and wakes everyone up. You can achieve the same effect by opening the window, burning a candle or vaporizing essential oils.

Moisten the air

Dry living rooms with central heating can block your nose and create a stuffy atmosphere. Place small bowls of water or commercial humidifiers under the radiators to act as air-conditioners

Buy second-hand furniture

Buying second-hand furniture is an environmentally sound form of shopping. You can often pick up great bargains, pieces that you wouldn't have been able to afford new. Visit auction centres (they aren't as frightening as they at first seem), house auctions and sales and second-hand or nearly new shops. Let your friends know that you wouldn't be averse to some extra furniture, and they'll often be only too happy to oblige. Don't be frightened of putting on a handle or fixing a hinge. Simple jobs can take you minutes and often save you money.

Lighting up the planet

Lighting in the living room is important. You can't afford to strain your eyes when you are reading, for example, but you can buy special lamps and clip-on lights that use compact fluorescent bulbs. Although they cost more initially, they will save you money within a year and cut carbon dioxide levels that cause global warming. Just eight ordinary light bulbs of 60 watts produce one tonne of carbon dioxide during their lifetime. It takes forty-six fluorescent bulbs to create the same amount of pollution.

Make your flowers last longer

Everyone wants cut flowers to last longer and look beautiful, and you don't have to use chemicals on them. I find that cutting the stems into an angle with a very sharp knife helps the flowers take more water. Be prepared to change the water and keep it topped up. Apparently the fungicidal properties of a brass pot or a penny keep the plants fresh for longer, although I haven't tried this myself.

Site your thermostat in your living room

The central heating thermostat controls the whole system and the temperature throughout the house. You could be making your system work overtime if it is positioned near windows or external doors which cool it down. The end result will be overheating in many rooms. Better to place the thermostat away from draughts in the room you use most often, such as the living room.

The Bedroom

Have a rainforest-free bedroom

Many bedrooms use wood for wardrobes, beds and drawers. Less expensive chipboard furniture is bonded with formaldehyde resins and may have hardwood veneers obtained from rainforests or plastic surfaces that attract dust and dirt. Solid-wood bed sources are easier to identify, and the beds will last longer, as they are sturdier.

Buy a sound bed

Your bed can be environmentally friendly. Buy a bed from sustainable forest sources. That means not buying hardwoods, but softwoods such as pine are fine. You can even find organic, animal-free waxes and varnishes to finish the bed and give you a green night's sleep.

Don't buy cheap foam mattresses

Foam mattresses can be fire hazards, releasing toxic cyanide fumes when burnt, but they also can contain CFCs, responsible for destroying the ozone layer. Go for natural fillings for your mattress instead. Concern has been voiced in West Germany and around Europe about magnetized spring coils in mattresses. Doing without them may help us to have a better night's sleep, as our nerves will not constantly have to readjust to the magnetic impulses from the springs.

Use a hot water bottle

There's something very comforting about a hot water bottle. It can warm more than your feet, and I've known it to help relieve period pains, cramps and the misery of 'flu. Use it instead of an electric blanket. Some evidence has emerged of an increase in the numbers of miscarriages among women who use electric blankets, and cancer is suspected.

Check your bedding

Rich, thick duvets and fleecy pillows can make your bed comfortable and warm, but do you know where they come from? Synthetic materials are made from petrochemicals, a non-renewable, non-biodegradable resource; some duvet fillings are made with traditional duck feathers, which are biodegradable but are increasingly taken from intensively reared ducks, kept in appalling conditions. You will have to make up your own mind before you can sleep easy in your bed.

Keep warm with natural fibres

Blankets with acrylic fibres are produced from acrylonitrile, which is a suspected human carcinogen. The chemical has been known to cause breathing difficulties and weakness in those sensitive to it. It might be better for your health to avoid such blankets and opt for those made from non-toxic alternatives such as pure wools and cottons.

Rest your head on a toxic-free pillow

Polyurethane foams used in pillows can be dangerous to your health. The foams are produced from petrochemical derivatives, and studies in the USA have found higher instances of bronchitis and skin problems among people who are in

contact with them. Polyurethane foams are known carcinogens in animals, but the main concern centres on their
behaviour in a fire. When mixed with polyester (often used
in pillowcases), they can produce toluene disocyanate, a
poisonous gas. Most deaths from fires occur because of smoke
inhalation, not burning, and having such foams in your home
will increase your risk of serious injury if there is a fire.

Buying an iron-free solution?

Some sheets and linens are sold on the basis of being 'easy-
care', 'no iron' or 'permanent press'. This usually means that

formaldehyde has been added. The manufacturing process ensures that the formaldehyde is permanent and will release its fumes continuously. It can aggravate asthma and cause coughing and streaming eyes. Mixtures of polyesters and cottons often have formaldehyde finishes. If you have suffered at night, it may be because of your sheets, so take a closer look at what you lie on.

The Hall

Use compact fluorescent lighting

The electric light was invented between 1878 and 1879 by a Briton and an American. Joseph Swan patented his light in 1878 in England and Thomas Edison his in 1879. They had both discovered how to use carbon to make a small heated filament glow. These first bulbs lasted only some 150 hours; now ordinary incandescents can last about 2,000 hours. Compact fluorescent lights are the same size as an ordinary light bulb but can last for at least 8,000 hours and only use one fifth of the energy for the same amount of light. If everyone in Britain replaced just one light bulb, it would reduce the need for one power station and save 8 million tonnes of carbon dioxide, one of the greenhouse gases, every year. Although they are more expensive initially, compact fluorescents can also save you money.

Spring-green your light bulbs

Lights attract dust and dirt, which in turn make your lighting less efficient, so at least twice a year dust and clean light bulbs all over the house.

Use outdoor lights rarely

Outdoor lights should be used only if they are really necessary, as in the case of potentially dangerous steps, a dark road or an unusually positioned front door. Uplighting for large houses is particularly wasteful. You should always use long-lasting, compact fluorescents. You could link them with a timer set to go on as dusk falls and to switch off when the sun comes up.

Insulate your letterbox

Draughts can whistle through your letterbox. You should think about insulating it with a brush or flap.

Use a letter opener

The average American receives 598 pieces of mail every year (most of that is what we call junk mail), and the figure for Britain is growing rapidly. Even if the mail you receive is not junk, you can make use of the envelopes and paper. Use a letter opener and collect the empty envelopes in one place.

I recycle the large ones and use small ones as notepaper for messages. Stamps can be collected and sent to help charities like Oxfam.

Reject junk mailings

When you join an organization, or you fill in a questionnaire in your local shop or high street, you could be unwittingly allowing yourself to be besieged by junk mail because your address may end up on a mailing list that is sold for profit. In America 100 million trees are cut down every year to be used for junk mail. When you join new organizations, ask them not to sell your address. Write to the mailing preference service to get your name removed from its lists. In the case of companies that persist in sending you their junk, I suggest sending it back to them without a stamp: they may start taking note of your requests more quickly!

Put a note on your front door to stop free newspapers

Millions of free local newspapers are dropped through our doors every week. You do not have to be on a mailing list to receive this unsolicited garbage; people are paid to deliver them straight to your door without using the postal system. My local freesheet has the audacity to look like a newspaper on the front page, with news stories and information, but open it up and every single page is filled with advertisements. Put a note on your front door: say NO to wasted paper. If freesheets still arrive, start writing letters, not just to them but to the real local press too.

Check your front door

Every year in Britain we buy 1.5 million doors made from

wood grown in tropical rainforests. For the front door you will need a hardwood, but it is best to buy from native sources. The Women's Environmental Network's Green Home had a British oak door, traditionally limed with no chemical treatments. Ask builders, DIY stores and builders' merchants where the wood comes from, and avoid chemical treatments if you can.

Buying from representatives

The 'Avon lady' has become synonymous with door-to-door selling in Britain and America. Avon has secured a large proportion of the make-up and beauty market with exclusive ranges not normally available in the shops. Avon's 100,000 representatives in Britain sell their products in a given area for the company. They are paid a commission on what they sell: there is no basic salary, no management or back-up facilities. American research has shown that Avon reps earn less than the Federal minimum wage. They are, basically, a free labour force for the company. Other products often sold on door-steps or in especially arranged parties are cleaning products, household goods, shower units and home improvements such as double glazing. Do not be taken in by the hype. Ask yourself if you really need the product offered. Ask representatives to call back in a week's time before you sign anything, so you can 'cool off' and decide without pressure.

Buy your doormat from a cooperative

Supporting cooperatives from developing countries is one way of ensuring that handicrafts, art and local industry are kept alive without exploitation. You can buy wallhangings, doormats, prints and handicrafts and know you are supporting businesses that care about workers and share the wealth

among them. Oxfam shops usually stock a wide range of
Third World products.

Recycle your newspapers

During 1987 the British public threw 1.6 million tonnes of its
newspapers away and recycled just 350,000 tonnes. Recycling
could have increased the percentage of British-based paper,
cut down on energy and pollution and created more jobs.
Instead the market for waste paper virtually collapsed as
prices and collections fluctuated. The real problem lies with
the paper industry and the Government. Save your newspapers for recycling, and if you have nowhere to send them,
start applying pressure. Why not share your newspaper with a
neighbour or read it in the library for free? Don't buy those
you don't really read, and request a recycling service to be
provided by your local council. Buy more recycled paper
products to support the market.

Do-It-Yourself

Assess the energy you use in your home

It is vital that you assess the energy that you use in your home before embarking on an energy-efficiency programme. You could save lots of cash by doing it right the first time. From your local energy-efficiency office get a leaflet that shows you how to carry out out a simple home-energy audit. Check your last four gas, electricity and oil bills to see where most of the money goes. You'll soon see that space and water heating is the most expensive, followed by light and appliances. Check to see whether you have draught proofing and insulation in the loft, on pipes and in cavity walls. Make a priority list of what to do.

Recycle rain

Now that the British water industry has been privatized, and with water metering soon to follow, all sorts of suggestions for better use of water resources have been made. One company has devised a new scheme not only to collect the 700,000 litres (400,000 gallons) of rainwater that falls on the average semi-detached house but also to purify and filter it under ultra-violet light, in order to remove all traces of bacteria and viruses, so that it can be re-used. The cost (at about £3,000) has a pay-back period of ten years, which may look appealing when higher water bills start coming in.

Use off-peak electricity

If you don't have gas central heating, you should choose the type of electric heater you use very carefully. Small bar-type heaters consume enormous amounts of energy and should be used as little as possible. You may be able to take advantage of off-peak electricity supplies, which are cheaper to run, as they use energy at night and store it for when you need it in the daytime. Contact your local electricity board for help and advice.

Stop heat escaping through your floor

Gaps in floorboards can help heat to escape. You can close the gaps with wooden beading, plastic wood, newspapers and even plaster. Several newspapers laid flat under a carpet can act as an underlay and help to prevent heat loss. They will make your carpet seem thicker too. Wall-to-wall carpeting prevents heat loss through the floor.

Use the sun to heat your home

If you are lucky enough to have south-facing windows, you can use the sun to help heat your home. Open curtains and doors in sunny rooms, and let the gentle heat fill the rest of the house. You may find that you can turn down the heating in these rooms to save extra energy.

Fit a thermostat

A thermostat with a time programmer for your central heating could save you up to 20 per cent of your present fuel bills. That in turn means that you will save energy and reduce air pollution such as acid rain and carbon dioxide, which is given off by burning fossil fuels. Set the controls to fit in with the time you get up and go to bed at night. You can always override the clock if your schedule changes unexpectedly.

Control the heat in each room

By using thermostatic radiator valves you can set the temperature in each room at the desired level. This is very energy-efficient, especially if you use some rooms rarely. The valves require no electrical connections and can be fitted by any competent plumber or DIY enthusiast.

Make the heat from your radiators work for you

One simple way to make the heat from your radiators really effective is to fix ordinary kitchen foil on the wall behind them, so that the heat is reflected into the room rather than escaping through the wall. This is especially energy-saving for radiators on outside walls. For radiators under windows, try building a wide windowsill, which will help reflect the heat into the room. Don't let curtains hang over radiators either; you will just encourage the heat to escape through the window. Shorter curtains are a better solution.

Insulate water tanks and pipes

If you have just insulated your loft to save energy and money, you will find that the space in the loft will be colder. It is important that you insulate all the pipes and the cold water tank in your loft to stop them freezing up in winter.

Get an energy-saving grant

If you are on a low income, you should apply for a grant to insulate your home. The eligibility of a grant for home improvements changes often, and according to each local authority area, but it is worth asking your council or the social services department. You could get financial help to save precious pounds.

Draught-proof your windows

As much as 25 per cent of the heat in a British house can be lost through draughts, and a good deal of that slips through ill-fitting windows, sashes and locks. You can fit durable plastic strips for very little, generally about 15p per metre. For very narrow gaps and uneven windows use silicone rubber sealant, which is very cheap, although you may find that it cannot cope with seasonal changes easily.

DIY double-glazing

Double-glazing is expensive. Penny for penny, it does not make financial sense simply as a means to save energy, unless you are replacing your windows anyway or have already insulated the rest of the house. Double-glazing will muffle external noise and cut heat loss, but it may take up to twenty years to recoup the cost. But you can create do-it-yourself double-glazing: tack plastic sheeting into place around your windows. This is extremely cheap and effective, and its cost will be recouped within a few weeks. You will probably have to take it down in warmer weather.

Use cavity-wall insulation

Cavity-wall insulation means filling the cavity or gap between your walls with an insulating material. About 60 per cent of British houses have cavity walls; most have no insulation. You will have to find an experienced contractor to do the job for you. The cost is between £300 and £600, depending on the size of the house, but the pay-back period is about four years. This type of insulation is cheaper than most others, but you should avoid ureaformaldehyde (UF) foams, which can leak gases into your house, or foams containing chloro-fluorocarbons, which destroy the ozone layer.

Turn down the heat

If all the households in the USA lowered their heating by about 3°C (6°F) for a twenty-four-hour period, the equivalent of 570,000 barrels of oil could be saved. It doesn't make sense to heat a home to excess. Good insulation, lighting and thermostats will keep your house at a pleasant temperature. A 1°C reduction in the temperature of the average British home could save up to 8 per cent of its energy bill. Don't reduce temperatures below 18–20°C (64–8°F), though, particularly if you are elderly.

Forget the chandelier

Unless you live in a stately home, you are not really going to have much call for a real chandelier, but many people do have multi-bulb lighting, which uses expensive and wasteful numbers of specialist bulbs. You could cut out one or two of the bulbs, but it would be far better to change to a different type of lighting and discourage the use of multi-bulb lights.

Write to the Government about saving energy

Saving energy in the home is one of the most important ways to protect the environment. Every kilowatt hour of electricity produces 1 kilogram of carbon dioxide, which causes global warming. Every therm of gas produces more than 5 kilograms of carbon dioxide. The Government publishes leaflets and distributes information about cutting energy, although it has cut back on energy-saving programmes drastically in years. By writing to your MP you can show that you care about energy efficiency as an issue.

Use only pure white spirit as a paint remover

Commercial paint removers contain methylene chloride or dichloromethane, a chlorinated hydrocarbon solvent. It is dangerous to those with heart diseases, and the caustic will burn your skin within seconds of contact. No data are available to indicate the extent of environmental damage after the solution is washed down your sink, but it has been shown to be carcinogenic in animals. These products should be used only in well-ventilated rooms and never near naked flames, as the vapours give off phosgene, which is extremely toxic.

Use white spirit as a paint remover and water-based paints wherever possible.

Don't get into a sticky mess with glue!

The industrial processes used to manufacture glues and resins used by millions of DIY enthusiasts cause great concern to environmentalists. Solvents like methyl ethyl ketone, carbon disulphide methylene chloride, cyanacrylate and epoxy resin adhesives in general can cause pollution where they are manufactured as well as causing dizziness, numbness and rashes. One case study undertaken by the London Hazards Centre found that a bricklayer who used an epoxy resin adhesive suffered badly from nerve damage in his legs and from epoxy dermatitis (red itchy rashes) on his hands and neck. It was months before the rash cleared up, and the man is still suffering from circulatory problems. Do use organic glues and adhesives such as those made by Auro, and always wear gloves.

Green up your walls

Wallpaper originated in France in the fifteenth century as a cheap substitute for richly woven tapestries. Decorated with stencilled or hand-painted designs, it became very popular after the rise of paper mills around Europe. These days we buy billions of rolls of wallpaper for our homes and offices. If you are environmentally conscious, you may prefer to avoid wallpaper with plastic laminates and formaldehyde resins, and may even consider painting your walls instead of using precious paper. Painted walls are easier to keep clean and bright and do not need to be redecorated as often. If you want to introduce colours and patterns, stencilling is a very cheap and easily mastered alternative to wallpaper.

Do not buy asbestos cement

The production of most asbestos materials is prohibited for health reasons, but asbestos cement still slips through the net because it is cheap and people are fooled into believing that the fibres cannot escape into the air. It is used mostly for corrugated sheet roofing, walls of sheds and internal wall panels in flats, cold-water storage tanks, lining and shelves in cupboards, weather boarding, decking tiles for flat roofs and sheeting for fire doors. Asbestos cement causes problems at every stage of its production, use and disposal. The water supply may be contaminated; asbestos causes cancers in humans; people who work with it suffer from an increased risk of death from lung diseases. There is no 'safe dose'. The erosion of buildings by acid rain is causing even more problems, as the asbestos fibres are washed out or released into the air. The Fraunnhofer Institute in Germany estimates that 1 square metre (just over 10 square feet) of asbestos cement may release 1,000 million asbestos fibres an hour. The London Hazards Centre and the General and Municipal Boilermakers Union are calling for an immediate asbestos ban, as safe alternatives exist for every single use. Companies producing this deadly hazard are increasing production in developing countries. Do not buy it: boycott it.

Ban wood preservatives from your house

Pesticides, used as wood preservatives, can last for twenty or thirty years, which is why you can get timber-treatment guarantees for so long. Nearly all are suspected carcinogens and some, like Dieldrin, have been banned for a long time in the USA, only recently in Britain. Pentachlorophenol (PCP) has been blamed for over 1,000 deaths worldwide; just 3 grams of Lindane is a lethal dose; and tributyle tin oxide (TBTO) is a nerve poison. These chemicals and others are sprayed regularly in our homes (over 3 million British homes have been sprayed), and they are now widespread in the air, in water and in soil. Cancer-causing preservatives should be banned immediately, and other chemicals should be used with extreme caution, following strict safety and health guidelines.

Look after the bats in your roof

One of the main problems for bats in country areas is the spraying of chemical wood-preservative treatments in roofs, which can kill them. While no treatment can be absolutely safe, the Nature Conservancy Council suggests using zinc naphthenate because of its relatively low toxicity. Other solvents in the preservative may be harmful, however, and you should carry out work on your roof only if you are sure that there are no bats in the roof space. Contact the Nature Conservancy Council before you start work.

Turn off lights that you are not using

It's as simple as that!

Weatherproof doors and windows

Cold air can pass through the tiniest crack. It can freeze a hall if the door or window is not draughtproofed. The energy leaking from North American windows in 1988 was estimated to be equivalent to 522,000,000 barrels of oil. You can be saving up to 10 per cent of your energy bills by simple and very inexpensive draughtproof stripping.

Try pure cork for insulation

Many insulating foams use chlorofluorocarbons, which damage the ozone layer. Others contain tiny particles of urea-formaldehyde foams. Use pollution-free and safe insulation materials. Always ask what they contain. Try pure farmed cork without chemicals.

Insulate your loft

If you have not already done it, insulating your loft could be one of the quickest and most cost-effective ways of saving energy and preventing pollution. The insulation should be 15 centimetres (6 inches) thick. If you have less than this, top it up. You can usually tell which houses have poor or no insulation – just look up at the roofs on a cold day in winter and note where pigeons have settled. The heat of badly insulated houses is wasted on warming the roof tiles. Insulation could save you as much as 25 per cent of your fuel bills.

Close off rooms you do not use

If you have more rooms than you need, think seriously about closing them off and switching off radiators. You could greatly reduce the area of your home that needs heating.

An organic end for flies

If flies are buzzing around your home or near your dustbins in summer, and your first reaction is to reach for some fly spray – stop! Not only are fly sprays packaged in aerosol cans but they also contain tetramethrin and phenothrin, both highly toxic to fish, aquatic life and bees. The production of these pyrethroids is considered by the World Health Organization to be 'moderately toxic', but a dose of 15 grams (0.5 oz) has killed a child. Citrus oil repels flies just as easily, and boiled sugar, syrup and water on strips of brown paper make a less toxic death trap. Use a fly swatter too. Keeping your home clean is also a good fly-repellent, as flies feed off grease, rubbish and old food behind refrigerators and cookers.

Paint everything green!

British DIY enthusiasts buy £1.5 billion worth of paint each year, often without knowing the content of the tins and the environmental effects they may have. Public concern about the levels of lead in paint has ensured that only a few companies now include it, but paint contains other toxins. Asbestos, chlorinated hydrocarbons, xylene and trichloroethylene are just some of the chemicals you should avoid. For your own safety, avoid breathing paint fumes or smoking cigarettes while painting. Where possible, buy water-based or non-toxic paints, which contain safe, organic ingredients.

Rent or borrow equipment

When it comes to specialist equipment, both Britain and America score high in sales of DIY equipment that uses a great deal of electrical power and may be used only once or twice. Why not rent or borrow equipment instead? Friends and neighbours can cut down on needless consumerism by swapping their equipment.

Do not buy electric when people-power does just as well

The more specialized and elaborate your DIY tool, the more likely it is that it will use electrical energy. Lawn mowers and electric screwdrivers are just two examples of tools that do jobs that could be done by people-power instead of electrical power. You will save money too.

Get rid of methyl chloroform

Methyl chloroform is used as a solvent in paints, adhesives and varnishes, and it is estimated that some 544,600 tonnes of it were used in 1985 alone. Methyl chloroform is an ozone destroyer and has an atmospheric lifetime of 8.3 years. Because it is relatively stable, it has been substituted as a solvent for some of the faster ozone depleters, but this has meant that production has increased. Ask about methyl chloroform. Don't buy DIY products that contain it: switch to safer alternatives.

Can you breathe?

Formaldehyde is a toxic gas found in ordinary household products such as glues, chipboards, plywoods and insulating foams. A study in the USA found that about one in five people is sensitive to the effects of formaldehyde; the symptoms include dizziness, allergic reactions and headaches. Increased exposure increases sensitivity, and the gas itself is highly toxic if inhaled. It has been proved to cause cancer in animals and is a suspected human carcinogen. You should avoid formaldehyde whenever you can. If you have to work with it or if it is already present in your home, keep your rooms well ventilated and wear a mask when fitting insulating fibreglass materials.

Convert your junk

Convert and restore junk to prevent pollution and safeguard resources. Make a door into an occasional table or desktop, or a wardrobe into a kitchen cupboard; swap legs and drawers; pick up junk from skips and design cheap furniture yourself. There are plenty of books on the subject, and it could become an absorbing hobby.

Don't use a blowlamp

A blowlamp may be a handy way to get rid of paint on wood, but burning it off will release toxic fumes if the paint contains lead. Use a water-based paint stripper instead, and choose organic paints when repainting.

Use solar power

Solar panels may look like futuristic, expensive gimmicks, but new designs are proving all the time that it pays to install them. One model can save you up to 70 per cent of your heating costs, yet costs only £1,500 to install. Solar panels are clean, safe and quiet. They have no moving parts that need maintenance, and they are made from silicon, the world's second most common element. Even in cloudy conditions they take energy from the sun, a free, renewable source that is available to everyone and causes no environmental damage. The sun is definitely one of the energy sources of the future.

Recharge your torch

One unit of electricity from the mains costs around 5 pence or 9 cents. Batteries in a torch make the cost work out at over £200 or $300. Buy a rechargeable torch, and use it only in emergencies.

Clean up the drains

Use washing soda crystals for the drains. They prevent blocked drains and stop you from putting nasty chemicals into the water system. You are bound to save on plumbers' call-out charges too.

Gardening

Collect rainwater to wash your car with

Car washing wastes precious and expensively treated water. Why not collect rainwater or old bathwater and use that to wash your car with? Cut down on the number of washes you give it too – you will have more time for important environmental action.

Don't always burn dead leaves and stalks

Moths and other insects spin tiny cocoons under dead plants in autumn. By burning the plants you could be destroying both valuable helpers and food for your garden. It is far better to make a compost heap and to burn only a small amount of garden refuse. Check underneath the bonfire for hedgehogs first, especially in November, when these creatures crawl under piles of leaves to hibernate.

Plant wild fruit trees

Avoid imported fruit trees. Ask at a nursery for information about native varieties, and restore heritage, beauty and wildlife to your garden.

Germinate your own seeds

Many trees will survive for longer if you germinate them from local seeds; they are more likely to be adapted to the climate and soil, and you will be conserving important local stock. The grafting or budding of fruit trees is an ancient practice, and there are plenty of books that contain instructions on how to do it.

Never use paraquat

Exposure to very small amounts of paraquat used as a garden pesticide can cause skin rashes, inflammation of the eyes and the delayed healing of wounds. It is banned in Finland and Sweden and restricted in the USA and Turkey. It is acutely toxic and has killed people even when they have spat it out. There is no known antidote.

Let the dandelions grow!

Dandelions, thistles, clover and nettles attract butterflies. With the removal of hedgerows, the loss of many wild plants and the increased use of pesticides, our gardens could become sanctuaries for butterflies, so set aside a section of your garden for one or all of these plants. (Dandelions are also tasty additions to salads.)

Plant nectar-sweet garden flowers

Honeysuckle, lilac, lavender, thyme, marigold and sweet william bring colour and beautiful scent to a garden. Butterflies are attracted to these flowers too.

Encourage hedgehogs

Slugs are a nuisance, but the chemical pellets you use to kill them can kill hedgehogs and other wildlife travelling through your garden as well. As many as ten hedgehogs may visit your garden in one evening. Encourage the hedgehog, which eats slugs.

Make your pond safe

Garden ponds can be a death trap for small mammals and children. Ensure that small animals can escape by building slipways of half submerged bricks or rocks around the edges of a pond. Spread coarse netting across it to protect small children.

Do not buy peat

Two million tons of rich, fertile peat is sold for gardens in Britain every year. Over the last fifteen years we have managed to dig up some 96 per cent of it: there are now only 25,000 acres of pure peat bogland left, housing a variety of plants, birds, mammals and insects, including rare beetles and mosses. One seventh of the world's blanket bog is in Britain.

Look for alternatives, such as manure from your compost heap. Do not buy peat for your garden.

Feed good peanuts to birds

Bluetits can eat a third of their own weight in peanuts, according to the Birdfoods Standards Association, but many are accidentally killed by well-meaning enthusiasts, who feed these birds old and musty peanuts, which are poisoned by aflatoxins. Strict guidelines on human consumption of peanuts operate in many countries, but few people are aware of the dangers of feeding mouldy peanuts to birds.

Paving crazy

Don't concrete over your garden – not even small areas. The concrete prevents vital solar energy from reaching the soil and so makes the earth underneath useless. Natural drainage is hampered. Concrete is not as durable as stone in any case. If you want to construct a path or patio, use stone, bricks, wood or slate. Encourage growth between the cracks. Check your local garden centre for inexpensive and attractive ideas.

Encourage birds

Hang feeding bags on trees, or set up a bird table and encourage birds to dine there. Be sure to place the table out of reach of cats. So much of our countryside has been ruined by pesticides and chemicals, drainage and levelling that our gardens could be real havens for migrating birds.

Bonfires can be a hazard

Don't light bonfires just for the sake of it. You shouldn't burn household rubbish or wood, as these may give off toxic fumes. Consider your neighbours: have they got washing on the line, or are small children playing near by? Check whether your bonfire will burn nearby trees or bushes.

Protect seedlings

Protect seedlings from weeds and insects by laying old carpet or underlay around them. Make small holes in the places where the seedlings will pop up.

Grow herbs

Fresh herbs add a certain quality to a garden and make an ordinary meal special. They are easy to grow, attract butterflies and bees, keep away slugs and often have medicinal properties. Try clary sage to perk up your life, lavender (my favourite) for pot pourri, chives, marigold, rosemary, marjoram, sage and thyme to eat.

Buy organic untreated seeds

Packets of seeds were first marketed in Philadelphia in the 1880s, when Washington Atlee Burpee started offering flower and vegetable seeds as food for the poultry that he sold. People wanted the seeds more than the poultry, however, and by the early 1900s he was offering over 200 varieties of vegetable and flower seeds. Today billions of packet seeds are bought all over the world. Use good producers like the Henry Doubleday Research Association, which sells seeds without fungicides and chemicals to help them grow. They will be much hardier.

Grow your own food

Home-grown food saves energy and eliminates waste, chemicals and artificial fertilizers (provided you do it organically, of course); it also provides majestic, mouthwatering meals.

Grow beans, broccoli, soya, cabbage and cucumber, garlic and onions, lettuce and tomatoes, parsnips and even melons. And why not try some of the more exotic vegetables, which perhaps you can't afford to buy from supermarkets, like mangetout and asparagus?

Sow native flowers

Encourage native flowers grown from seed collections provided by garden lovers in your neighbourhood. They will feel welcome in familiar conditions and will grow well. They will also cut down on packaging and transporting, and you'll know that they have not been sprayed with chemicals.

Attract birds

Bird groups and organizations will readily supply lists of the many flowers and shrubs that can be grown to attract a wide variety of birds into your garden. Plant cotoneaster for blackbirds and thrushes, for example, and thistles for goldfinches. Don't shoo birds away for eating fruit off the trees; they will take their part in the food chain by eating small mammals and insects galore. Tits especially love insects and not berries.

Compost for city dwellers

Those of you who haven't got a garden, or who want a compost quickly, should collect your household food waste, preferably chopped as small as possible, and tie it up in a black plastic bag. Place the bag in a sunny spot for a month and you should have a good store of rotting waste, best when you can still see the shape of the original organic matter and its colour is fairly dark.

Forgo the motorized mower

Lawn mowers were invented in England in 1830 by a factory worker called Edwin Budding. Larger versions of his device were pulled by horse around English stately homes (I have seen them in Delhi being pulled by cows). The motorized petrol- or electricity-guzzling mower of today is an expensive and wasteful gadget for most ordinary lawns; a hand-pushed model will do the job – and the effort required may prompt even the garden-proud to leave the grass to grow!

Set aside an area for nothing but wildlife

We are so obsessed with order and tidiness in the garden that we forget that chaos can be very productive. A wild corner will soon buzz with life, given encouragement, and provide a habitat for aphid-loving insects and mammals.

Green garden furniture

In summer your garden is an extension of your house, and some furniture is essential for a relaxed and congenial atmosphere. Traditional soft-wood and cast-iron seats need constant painting or treatment to keep them in good condition; the hardwoods used for some garden furniture come from tropical rainforests. Check on the source of your furniture before you buy it.

Choose companion plants

Companion plants are important to any organic gardener because they repel bugs such as aphids and feed neighbouring plants with trace minerals. Garlic and onions are great bug repellents, but they shouldn't be planted together. Sow onions next to carrots and garlic next to roses. Herbs deter slugs. Get organized about your garden before you start to plant and you will save yourself a lot of time weeding and thinking up non-organic ways of getting rid of pests.

Build a greenhouse

A greenhouse is a boon: it is a warm refuge on a chilly day and a perfect place to grow your seeds and keep tools and equipment. In it you can grow and protect plants that might not survive in the garden, especially when it's cold, and it is a home-made store for solar energy.

Dig everything

One of the most effective ways to give soil a new lease of life, create good drainage and discourage harmful insects that feed on roots is to dig it. It also gets your muscles working!

Leave your lawn alone

Carole Rubin, one of Canada's top organic gardeners, sums up our attitude to manicured gardens well when she says, 'If you want your lawn to look like a green rug, you're probably better off with a carpet.' You must be prepared, whether growing organically or not, to put up with buttercups, daisies and clover. Clover is useful, because it adds nitrogen to the soil, and very few other so-called weeds will actually harm the grass.

Plant wild flowers to attract butterflies

Plant buttercups, gentians in a rockery, knapweed in herbaceous borders, lady's smock at the edge of ponds or hemp agrimony to attract butterflies into your garden. Get seeds from reputable organic suppliers, and follow the instructions carefully, as these flowers are often slow to germinate.

Bring back the hoverfly

Although the adult hoverfly is content with pollen and nectar as food, the larvae have an appetite for greenfly and other aphids, which is good news for your garden. Plant dill and fennel to attract the hoverfly, and they will double as culinary and medicinal herbs. Marigolds and daisies are useful too.

Look after your lawn

One quarter of the earth's surface is covered by one of the earth's most important plants – grass. The grass family includes more than 7,000 different species, including corn, wheat, sugarcane, rice, millet and barley, though grass to most of us usually means a lawn in the garden. In the USA there are over 20 million acres of lawn, and the environmental impact of the chemical fertilizers, lime, potash and other substances that are spread on them is enormous. (It is estimated that over 1 million tonnes of chemicals are spread on American lawns alone.) Cut down on the chemicals and you'll reduce the pollution in your garden and protect the environment as well.

Adapt tools for the elderly

Gardening is a pleasurable experience for people of all ages, but sometimes the elderly or frail are hindered by the lack of equipment that is suitable for their needs. Don't be put off! Help the Aged says you should choose tools that are well-balanced, light and sharp. Use household items as cheap alternatives – for example, instead of a trowel use a flour scoop, a cup or a cut-down soft drinks container with a ready-made handle. If you can't get outside, window boxes, hanging baskets and pots will give you a fine display of flowers.

Keep bees

Bees are an important part of any garden. They promote cross-pollination of plants and flowers, and some can provide you with all the honey you need to replace your sugar. Luxurious and free, honey bees are a wonderful addition to a garden. There are over thirty types of bee, though garden bees are probably the ones you'll come across most often if you don't have a hive. They fly at lower temperatures than other species and live in holes in the ground. They have a special liking for compost heaps, and they don't sting readily, so don't try to harm them. Grow scabious, kidney vetch, yellow melilot, viper's bugloss and buttercups especially for them.

Start a compost heap

Compost is a panacea for any garden. It nourishes your soil and gives it a rich texture. Nurture your compost heap with left-over food, manure, leaves, garden debris and even newspapers (without coloured inks), but don't use it until the components have rotted thoroughly. With a compost activator (you can find organic ones) you could be using your mixture within six months. A compost heap will take care of about 30 per cent of your household waste, spare you from using chemical alternatives and save energy too.

Stick up for the earwig

Lindane is an insecticide that is used to kill earwigs. It's a persistent poison and has been blamed for the decline of bat populations; it is also especially poisonous to cats, which can't remove it from their bodies as efficiently as other animals. But the earwig is a much maligned creature, blamed for piercing eardrums and ruining prized flowers. In fact, it is a harmless vegetarian – though it can do some damage to flowers. Insecticide used on it will destroy other useful insects such as ladybirds, which eat greenflies, and will upset the garden ecosystem.

Look after garden tools

Your garden tools are valuable. Looking after them is vital for more reasons than just cost. A blunt blade will tear grass, and that will weaken it and attract weeds and disease. You can destroy roses by pruning with blunt secateurs. Don't buy tools with handles made from rainforest wood.

*

Dispose of garden chemicals carefully

If you have just decided to go organic, you may find that you have a selection of dangerous and poisonous herbicides and pesticides in your garden shed or greenhouse. The only expedient for most of us at the moment is to send them to our local councils for disposal. They should *never* be poured down a drain, as this would add more poisons to our already polluted water system.

Grow green manure

Green manure is composed of plants that are grown especially to feed the soil. They are generally fast-growing and produce a mass of weed-smothering foliage. Sown in winter, when the soil is idle, they capture the micro-organisms released in the autumn and store them for the spring, protecting the soil from frost at the same time. Grow mustard, rye, fenugreek and clover.

Save water

The average North American gardener overwaters his or her lawn by up to 40 per cent, which wastes over 45,000 litres of water for every 0.4 hectare of lawn (10,000 gallons per acre). Overwatering is an easy way to destroy your lawn and use up precious summer supplies. You could save a quarter of the water used in the home each summer if you gave up watering the lawn altogether, but if you must, use sprinklers and hoses in the evening, when the water will evaporate much more slowly. Don't water lawns in droughts. Grass that is going brown will recover after rain falls again. The water is crucial for more basic needs.

*

Prepare your soil

Pest-resistant plants and lawns need a good healthy soil. You may need to feed your garden a regular diet of organic fertilizers to keep it healthy. Test your soil, and get guidance and help from the many books and reports that are available. The importance of this cannot be overstated.

Choose organic fertilizers

Fertilizers put back into your garden what plants and the rain take out of it. They are vital for the well-kept garden, as all plants will die eventually if they are 'starved' of nutrients. The three main nutrients a garden needs are nitrogen, potassium and phosphorus, but it may also need calcium, iron, zinc and magnesium in small quantities. Organic fertilizers contain fish and blood meal, kelp meal and wood ash as well as compost, your garden's richest and cheapest food if you make it yourself.

Build a bat box

All British bats are harmless, and they can devour thousands of insects in an evening. Bats are protected by law, and you can encourage them to use your garden by building a bat box. Contact your local conservation group for ideas and help.

Feed your birds well

Don't feed birds artificial food, such as bread and nuts, after March. This food isn't usually nutritious enough for young birds in spring. They will mostly feed on worms and berries during spring and on artificial foods such as nuts, apples, suet and oats (bread should be soaked) during winter. Don't feed them desiccated coconut, which swells inside them and can

kill them. Encourage spring food by planting trees and shrubs, which in turn produce berries and seeds and support an insect population.

Provide shelter for birds

Birds often need some help in finding a home, especially as the numbers of trees are dwindling. Plant evergreens, holly or a thick hedge for shelter in winter, and persuade all kinds of birds to remain in your garden by providing boxes.

Build a pond

A pond in your garden will set you apart from other gardeners. It will attract frogs and water beetles, and you will be able to watch birds around the edges and goldfish eating mosquito larvae. Use hardwearing butyl rubber as a base for an inexpensive sheet-formed pool. Plant pond plants as oxygenators and floaters to prevent the build-up of algae.

Get rid of aphids organically

It is counter-productive to use insecticide to kill aphids. It generally kills too the predator animals that would otherwise get rid of these pesky insects for you. A soft-sud mixture of environmentally safe washing-up liquid will remove their waxy layer and make them shrivel up and die. Grow plants to attract aphid lovers, especially ladybirds. Get advice from organic garden centres. Whatever you do, don't use strong pesticides like lindane or captan, as these are banned in other countries because of their toxicity.

Check out your weeders

A conventional garden guide I've just bought still suggests 2,4-D as a weedkiller, as it is effective against many annual and perennial weeds. Yet evidence shows an increasing chance of developing a rare form of cancer among farmworkers in the USA who use it.

Mulch it

If you don't fancy digging, why not mulch your garden? Mulching could increase your vegetable yields by as much as 50 per cent, and it's easy to do. Just flatten weeds and flowers in autumn, cover with a thick layer of compost or well-rotted manure and cover over with newspapers or old carpet (even black plastic bags). By spring you will find a wonderful, rich soil for planting in.

Plant holly around shrubs and bushes

Holly around your shrubs and bushes keeps cats away, as they don't like the prickly leaves. Birds can tolerate them quite happily, however, so offer them the protection of holly.

Grow by the moon

Sowing seeds before a new moon encourages root growth because there is a stronger gravitational pull to the earth. This stabilizes the plant and increases its chance of survival. Transplanting and cutting at the time of a full moon encourages better leaf development, and the properties of herbs and vegetables are said to be richer.

Convert your nettles

Nettles are weeds with many uses. Five hundred species are found all over the world, but the common stinging nettle occurs widely in temperate climates like Britain's. Although you can be stung by this herbal weed, it has been used in the past as a tonic, because it has a high vitamin content, and as a drink to clear the lungs and chest of phlegm. Nettles in your garden are the sign of a rich, fertile soil. Collect them and put them into an airtight container. Cover with water and leave for four to six weeks. Use undiluted as a pesticide and diluted with ten parts of water as an incredibly rich fertilizer. And it's free!

Fool them with marigolds

Marigolds are wonderful for fooling aphids. Their smell masks the scent of the aphids' favourite flowers (and also stops dogs and cats from jumping on your flowering borders). Greenfly are completely fooled, which could save the rest of your flowers.

Elderberry or rhubarb mix as a weapon against aphids

About 1.8 kilograms (4 pounds) of elderberry or rhubarb leaves boiled with 4.5 litres (1 gallon) of water for one and a half hours make a superb organic pesticide. Add a teaspoon of ordinary soft soap, so the mixture will remain on leaves, and use as a thin liquid spray against aphids.

Beer gardens work

Half fill an old tin can with beer and dig it into the ground. Slugs will be instantly attracted to this treat, and you'll be able to collect dozens of them in the morning without having to resort to chemicals at all.

Root it organically

To promote root growth in plants without using fungicides, why not use an ancient organic method? Cut branches of willow and steep them in water for between six and twenty days. The resulting mixture is an organic rooting hormone,

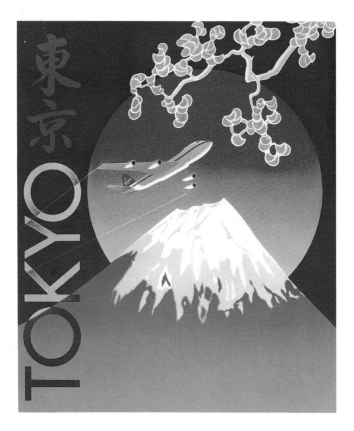

VIRGIN

POST CARD

SERIES

CLASSIC POSTER

AFFIX
STAMP
HERE

Reservation Numbers U.K. 0293 747747
U.S. Toll Free 1 800 862 8621; Tokyo 03 5269 2680
– or see your travel agent –

Virgin atlantic

excellent for fuchsias or similar hardwood plants. You have only to dip the cuttings in to promote root growth. The mixture is deadly, so keep children and pets away and label very carefully.

Plant nasturtiums

Climbing nasturtiums have edible flowers but are also useful if you want to attract blackflies away from your cucumbers. These pests will be attracted to the back of the nasturtium leaves, so your vegetables can enjoy some peace.

Pets and the Environment

Use pennyroyal to get rid of fleas

Pennyroyal is a member of the mint family and was first used by the Romans to drive away fleas. You can use dried pennyroyal leaves packed in your cat's or dog's collar, or wash your pet frequently in pennyroyal oil to ward off these annoying insects. Don't go to the expense of using artificially created fleabanes, which often contain toxic organophosphate compounds and are the cause of most fatal cases of poisoning among pets.

Don't buy exotic birds

Europe and North America are the biggest markets for wild birds. Poorer countries are encouraged to catch and sell millions of parrots, macaws, cockatoos, flamingos, budgerigars and birds of prey. Some are endangered species, and nine out of ten die before they reach their destination. They are crammed into crates in plastic tubes, without adequate food or water. Their own body heat often suffocates them. Many others die waiting in quarantine. These exotic birds are not pets; they should be allowed to fly about in their natural habitat without persecution.

Oppose the giving of live animals as prizes

At fairgrounds, bazaars and fêtes prizes often include live pets such as goldfish. These fish are stressed and suffer from oxygen starvation, the main cause of their death. A minute change in water temperature can kill a goldfish instantly, and tipping them out of polythene bags into bowls of tap water when you get home can be fatal. They need room-temperature water and should never be kept in small goldfish bowls, which do not provide them with the oxygen they need. Don't accept a goldfish as a prize, and encourage fairground traders to adopt ideas that are more ecologically sound.

Keep your pony or horse in the countryside

A pony is the second most popular pet for a young child, whether in countryside or town. Although there are over a hundred types of horse and pony in the world, the great majority of ponies in Britain descend from just nine moorland breeds. They are sensitive and highly strung animals with a strong herd instinct, and they ought to be kept in the countryside with companions. The RSPCA reports a worrying trend in the practice of keeping ponies in urban areas. They need to have at least 1 hectare (2.5 acres) of land and a box.

Don't buy a throw-away pet

Each Christmas the RSPCA and rescue homes like the Battersea Dogs' Home are taking in more and more pets – unwanted gifts. Strays and those left at rescue homes, however, account for only a small percentage of the animals (especially dogs) that roam the streets. If you think you want a pet, consider the matter carefully, and buy one only if you know that you will be able to give it time for exercise and attention. Over 1 million dogs were put down in Britain last year. Don't give other people pets as presents unless you are certain of their commitment.

Train your dog to use the gutter

A puppy is old enough to be house-trained at eight weeks old, and it usually takes about a month for it to be fully trained. It wouldn't take much longer to train a dog to use the gutter – yet a surprising number of dog owners don't seem to be concerned about foul pavements. Clean up the streets. Train your dog.

Use garlic

Garlic is an important food for human beings, but it can be useful for animals too. Pet lovers recommend garlic as a non-toxic and safe alternative to chemical tablets for getting rid of worms in cats and dogs. Mix raw garlic with their food.

Don't let your pet annoy the neighbours

Keeping a dog in a city can be a problem for the dog, which may not get out as much as it needs to, and for the neighbours, who have to put up with barking. If you have a dog, you have a responsibility to look after it and stop this annoying form of noise pollution whenever possible. Plenty of walks and exercise should keep your dog happy.

Consider hens for your garden

Keeping hens in your garden, if it's big enough, is a wonderful alternative to dogs and cats. They can be fed on grains and scraps from the kitchen and will produce fresh organic eggs for you as well as manure for your garden. Cockerels can be noisy, however, if you are not in the country. Think carefully before getting one.

Say no to the tropical aquarium

Tropical fish come mostly from freshwater sources in tropical countries and are exported for sale around the world. They are difficult to breed in captivity, and about 60 per cent of imported tropical fish die within a year of purchase. Tanks for these fish are often too small, and chlorinated water affects them. Exotic aquatic life should be left in its real home.

Give your pets a healthy diet

Dogs and cats today eat a very unhealthy diet. The tinned food that we buy them contains sugars, stimulants and preservatives to which the animals may become addicted. The cans may be contaminated with lead, and the meat inside is unfit for human consumption, which is why it's fed to our pets. Dogs and cats should ideally be fed on the raw organs of their prey. Although they will hate the diet at first, a raw-fed animal will be far healthier in the long run. But such food is almost impossible to procure, so careful thought is necessary when it comes to planning a pet's diet. Although cats need about three-quarters of their diet to be meat, dogs can survive on just one-third meat, the balance to be made up by grains, scraps and vegetables. Alternatively, dogs can be raised as vegetarians from birth; vegetarian organizations will give you advice about suitable foods. Cats and dogs seem to suffer less from parasites when on a healthy diet, so you may find vet bills cheaper too.

Put a bell on it!

Cats are responsible for killing at least 10 million birds in Britain each year. Help to reduce these deaths by putting a bell around their necks, the louder the better. If possible, in summer and during the breeding season don't let your cat out between first light and 8.30 a.m. and at dusk. Parent birds are busy finding food for their fledgelings and are most distracted at these times.

Personal Greening

Hygiene and Beauty

Be assertive

When we shop for beauty products in large department stores, we're often approached by well-groomed sales assistants in clinical white coats, who look like trained beauticians, dermatologists or chemists. They are not. They are there purely to sell you goods. At least one-third of the beauty products and treatments we buy are bought from these assistants and are purchased because customers are not assertive enough to say no. We are buying products we don't really need, wasting resources and energy.

Make your own hairspray

Modern hairsprays come in aerosols and contain a wide variety of synthetic chemicals, including cancer-causing polyvinylpyrrolidone plastic (PVP), formaldehyde, artificial perfumes and alcohol. Hairsprays are extremely flammable and often carry warning labels about the consequences of accidental inhalation or spraying into eyes. If you really must use hairspray, why not try making your own? One recipe suggests using whole lemons chopped and boiled in water until half the mixture is left. Strained and cooled, and applied to clean hair, it can make an effective alternative to manufactured sprays. Refrigerate the mixture in a pump-action container for a cheap, safe, non-toxic spray.

Banish the varnish

Nail varnish and nail-varnish remover are subtle mixtures of toxic chemicals. Phenol, toluene, formaldehyde and xylene are the main ingredients. Prolonged exposure to chemicals such as xylene affects the nervous system, and chemical reference books suggest avoiding skin contact. Healthy nails need contact with the air. You'll have to banish the varnish. Sorry: there are no green alternatives.

Go for an ammonia-free permanent wave

Hair-perm solutions generally include ammonium thioglycolate (or thioglycollate), which is highly toxic if you swallow or inhale it. It causes rashes and swelling, and it can be absorbed through the scalp into the bloodstream. The ammonia can also make breathing difficult, so look for an ammonia-free product and ask your hairdresser to use it on your hair.

Dye your hair green

Hair colourings are generally extremely dangerous. Some are known carcinogens, although loopholes in American regulations prevent the Food and Drug Administration from issuing warnings about them. They contain ammonia, detergents, ethanol, glycols, colours and fragrances, hydrogen peroxide, lead and sulphur compounds. In Britain there are no regulations governing their use, and complete lists of ingredients do not appear on the packets. Unless you are absolutely certain about their contents, it is better to stick to natural substitutes like henna or paprika for red hair, ginger, hot coffee or nutmeg for brown, chamomile or ceylon tea for honey.

Crunch a clove for fresh breath

Don't be fooled into thinking you need a mouthwash containing ammonia, hydrogen peroxide, ethanol and formaldehyde to make your breath fresh. This is not the answer to your problem. Try crunching a clove, brushing your teeth and changing your diet first. If that fails, see a dentist.

Buy cruelty-free

Every year over 20 million animals die agonizing deaths in tests conducted in the cause of profit around the world. New beauty products, perfumes, lipsticks, nail varnishes, talcum powder, hairspray and eyeshadows are tested on dogs, rabbits, chimps and rats. Pellets of lipstick are force-fed to laboratory animals to test lethal dosages. Shampoos and lotions are dripped into rabbits' eyes to test their effects, and, as rabbits cannot blink or cry, they are unable to restrict the pain they products on the market today, so there is no longer any need to buy cosmetics that have been tested on animals.

Say no to musk oil from deer

Glands in the male musk deer secrete one of the most valuable fluids in the world – musk oil. To obtain 1 kilo (2.2 lb) of musk, forty adult males have to be killed. In 1986 it was reckoned that 37,000 of these endangered animals were killed world-wide, mostly illegally. Because of the scarcity of the deer, more than 300 synthetic chemicals have now replaced the real thing. Animal rights groups say that some perfumes still contain deer musk, including 'Chanel No. 5', Guerlain's 'L'Heure Bleue' and Rochas' 'Madame Rochas'. International legislation protects the musk deer, but evidence from the World Wildlife Fund shows that Japan and France are still importing oil, about 80 per cent of which is thought to be illegally obtained.

Do you need a moisturizer?

The skincare market is worth an estimated £40 million a year in Britain alone and is growing fast. Prices for moisturizers range from 50 pence to £50 for 28 grams (1 oz). Most dermatologists insist that there is little difference between them. One of the world's leading dermatologists, Professor Albert Kligman, suggests that you should use only two products, petroleum jelly and a good sunblock. Don't waste your money on packaging.

Ignore the hype

Forget the wild claims made for creams and lotions that will change your skin, repair DNA cells, remove wrinkles and make you look ten years younger. In Britain we spend

£1,500 million a year on beauty products, and most of that money is claimed by advertising and marketing, very little by the product itself. The marketing relies on pseudo-scientific language that proves nothing at all about the benefits of the products. Ignore the hype. Look for alternatives that don't cost a fortune (try wheatgerm oil for wrinkles, for example).

Don't use lead-based eye make-up

Surma, an Asian eye make-up that is usually lead-based, is poisonous, especially to children. In 1985 the British Government issued strong health warnings about it, but most of it comes into Britain through friends and relatives, not through shops. The continued use of lead in make-up is an environmental problem as well as a serious health risk.

Wear greener lipstick

Lipstick is an oily product based on lanolin, petroleum jelly, silicone wax, castor oil and perfume, as well as colour pigments, usually eosin. The colours known as FD and C Red No. 2 are banned in the USA but not in the UK. Titanium dioxide is a white pigment used to make pink and opaque shades. The continued manufacture of titanium dioxide has provoked campaigns by Greenpeace, as the waste effluent causes serious environmental problems around the British coastline. Buy lipstick without the dangerous chemicals and always cruelty-free.

Buy cruelty-free eye make-up

Most eye make-ups, mascaras, eye-shadows, eyeliners and eye pencils are tested on animals unless the label says otherwise. The Draize eye test is particularly cruel, as it is used on animals that can't cry or blink. Some eye make-ups even

contain animal ingredients. If you want to avoid these, go for
products from the Body Shop or Beauty Without Cruelty,
for example.

Avoid skin whiteners

In the 1960s the cosmetics and perfume industries identified a
new market: catering for people with black skin. One of the
more alarming products that came on to the market was
mercury-based skin-lightening soap. This can cause severe liver
and kidney trouble, not to mention the environmental problems arising from continued use of mercury. Although mercury soap is banned in Britain, in 1985 a London-based
company was fined for producing the soap, which they
claimed was only for export to Africa.

Reduce your use of perfume

The world spends an amazing $2 billion on fragrances every
year (£400 million in the UK alone), which makes the perfume
industry one of the biggest beauty industries in the world.
We pay most of that money for packaging and advertising.
Parfums Internationaux spent $10 million on promoting its
'Passion' perfume. Every year about fifty new brands come
on to the market, mostly after extravagant launches. Perfume
is the main ingredient in many products that cause rashes and
allergies. Some scents are photosensitive (react to sunlight)
and cause irritation when worn in the sunlight. But perfume
can have an uplifting psychological effect on us: why not try
perfume from refillable bottles, not tested on animals, or pure
essential oils?

Cut out the coral

Coral jewellery looks beautiful, but the world's coral reefs are being endangered by overfishing, waste dumping and the trade in trinkets, including bracelets, necklaces and rings. Coral reefs support one-third of all fish species: it is their home that is being slowly destroyed around the world. Cut out the coral.

Perspire with nature

Ninety-two per cent of American women and 86 per cent of American men use deodorants. The vast and profitable business of producing alternatives to our body odour is quite out of proportion to the number of people who have real body odour. Anti-perspirants and deodorants contain substances such as aluminium chlorohydrate, formaldehyde and ammonia, and chemically produced perfumes and fragrances are also included. They are usually packaged in that wasteful tin, the aerosol. Aluminium is probably the most dangerous ingredient of these products. In anti-perspirants it works by blocking the pores in the skin to prevent sweating. Deodorants do not stop sweat: they change the smell. Many people have suggested baking soda as the most effective alternative, but regular washing helps considerably. If your body odour is offensive, you might try looking at your diet or your lifestyle. Sweating is the body's way of expelling poisons; you may have to look into your intake of these poisons, especially in your diet.

Say no to badger bristles for shaving

Badger bristles are regarded as the best bristle for shaving brushes. Badgers are now a rarity in the British countryside because of badger baiting, hunting and loss of the badger's natural habitats, woodland and hedgerows. There are many good alternatives that last just as long. We do not need to use badgers to get a clean shave.

Wind up your watch

Instead of using battery-operated watches and clocks, why not use an old-fashioned wind-up? It is much cheaper, and its simple technology means that it will last for years.

Soften your nails naturally

To soften the cuticles of your nails use olive oil instead of synthetic chemical formulae. It needs to be applied only once a week.

Clothes

Buy well-fitting shoes that will last

We buy about 200 million pairs of shoes every year in Britain, often ones that do not fit our feet. Rather than buy several pairs for just a year or two, choose shoes that will last and that fit properly. Believe it or not, 45 per cent of North American women wear uncomfortable shoes for the sake of fashion, and at least 20 per cent North American men do the same. Do yourself a favour: insist on shoes that fit your feet, not the latest fashion.

Do less ironing

Irons were used by the Greeks as long ago as the fourth century BC but it was not until 1882 that the first electric iron was invented. It was used by the ever-growing number of households in North America that had access to electric light fittings, the sockets of which could be used as plugs. Ironing uses a great deal of energy, which in turn produces carbon dioxide, adding to the greenhouse effect. Most clothes do not need ironing at all (some people still iron their underwear and hankies!). Save yourself a lot of bother – keep ironing to a minimum. Avoid heating and reheating the iron by planning your ironing sessions. Steam irons use much more energy than dry irons.

Wear more clothes when it gets colder

There are people who insist on wearing summer clothes throughout the year and turn up the central heating in winter. This costs energy, increases pollution and is more expensive. In cold weather you should wear warm clothing that retains your body heat instead of trying to create warmth artificially.

Do not use mothballs

Mothballs are made with 1,4 dichlorobenzene or paradichlorobenzene and naphthalene, which are highly toxic if swallowed. Studies have found cancers caused by these substances in laboratory animals. They are extremely persistent in the environment, and long-term exposure to them can cause kidney and liver damage. Using mothballs means that you spread the vapours and particles of this chemical through your clothes continuously. Try lavender bags for a safer, cheaper alternative. Keep your clothes clean to stop the build-up of moth eggs.

Dry clothes on the line

The ultimate clothes drier and sterilizer is the sun. If you have a garden or balcony, by far the best way to dry clothes is on a line outside. A tumble drier uses 3 kWh of electricity to dry 4 kilograms (8.8 lb) of clothing, which costs money and causes extra pollution.

Buying shoes from rainforests?

Some of the leather used to manufacture the 188.7 million pairs of leather shoes imported annually by Britain comes from South America. Leather is one of the by-products of the cattle-ranching industry, which is destroying vast areas of tropical rainforest. Although South American countries desperately need the income to pay back their foreign debt, take a closer look next time you buy shoes, and go for shoes made closer to home.

Use alternative bleach

The sun is our most ecologically friendly bleaching agent. It also sterilizes. But if the sun is not shining, you can use sodium percarbonate, which is made from salt, limestone and hydrogen peroxide, in preference to chlorinated bleaches. Skip the optical brighteners in soap powders; they simply fool you into thinking that something is cleaner than it is. Sodium perborate works only at high temperatures. Ecover, the alternative soap manufacturer, estimates that 50,000 tonnes of perborate is wasted every year in Britain on washing nonwhites and at temperatures below 60°C (140°F). Use a bleach in your wash only when you really need it, and choose a safer alternative.

Use a greener fabric softener

Fabric softeners were invented purely to reduce the static that builds up on synthetic fibres. Clever marketing and advertising have led us to think that we need them for every item of clothing. They leave on all fabrics a residue of chemicals that has caused allergic reactions in many people. The softeners also break down the natural oils in jumpers and help them to get dirtier. Try using a quarter of a cup of white vinegar in the final rinse if you really need a fabric softener.

Remove spots with soap flakes

Most spots and stains can be eased off with a good scrub with soft soap flakes and warm water before you put the clothes in the wash. Do not spend money on harmful and wasteful chemicals.

Get your own spray starch

Aerosol cans of spray starch, which adds body to shirts, are generally highly toxic products. They may contain formaldehyde, pentachlorophenol and phenols and are corrosive and dangerous if they touch the skin. They also give off toxic fumes when heated. Try dissolving one tablespoon of cornflour in 1.1 litres (1 pint) of water, shake and spray from a refillable spray bottle.

Avoid dry-cleaning

Solvents used for dry-cleaning are known to cause health and environmental problems. Perchloroethylene is irritating to the eyes and throat in concentrated amounts and gives off toxic fumes when heated. It is toxic in water and should never be disposed of down the sink. Some solvents are known to damage the ozone layer and should be banned completely. You can minimize the risk by not buying dry-clean-only garments.

Be ruthless about clothes shopping

We all buy clothes we don't really want. It is estimated that in Britain alone we have over £30 billion worth of clothes stuffed away in wardrobes and drawers, unworn and unwanted. Be ruthless when you go shopping for clothes. It doesn't make sense to buy clothes that don't fit (when exactly are you going to lose/gain that weight?). Don't buy clothes you don't need just because they are in a sale.

What's on your legs?

Women have been wearing stockings since AD 600, when soft leather *sykhos* covered their legs in Greece. The latinized *soccus* became the forerunner of the 'sock' and was brought from Rome to the British Isles. Early British stockings were made of silk, but these days some 500 million pairs of tights per year are made of nylon. The nylon stocking was invented by the chemical company Du Pont in the USA in 1938, and in the first year 3 million pairs were sold. They did seem to last longer than silk at first, but nowadays the average woman uses twenty-five pairs of nylon tights per year. They were not biodegradable and are often linked to health problems like thrush. Wear cotton tights or socks more often, or enjoy bare legs.

Phase out fashion

High-fashion clothes are produced four times a year. Colours, trends, shapes and sizes are altered to get you to update your wardrobe continuously in line with the latest fashion. Fashion is an important part of our culture, but it has become a hyped marketing strategy to persuade naive customers to buy billions of items every year. Classic clothes that are well made stay in fashion longer because they don't need fads to sell them. Don't buy just for fashion's sake.

Buy an energy-efficient washing machine

The energy we need to wash our clothes in Britain produces over 3.5 million tonnes of carbon dioxide, the main greenhouse gas. If you have to buy a new washing machine, choose one that is energy-efficient. If we all did this, we could reduce the carbon dioxide levels produced by over 60 per cent. The US Government has standardized energy labelling on all electric goods, and customers can calculate savings before they buy them. Most companies produce detailed information about their models, but you have to beg showroom assistants to part with it! Do your homework, and you could save a lot of money and cut down on pollution.

You don't need animal-tested clothes

The clothing industry uses animals in a subtle way. The production and processing of fur, leather, wool, cotton and synthetics requires the use of animal-tested chemicals, animal-tested drugs and vaccines and animal-tested bleaches, dyes and pesticides. Say no to animal-tested clothing. Watch out for the growing number of businesses that can guarantee animal-free clothes.

Oppose the fur trade

Fur coats are luxury garments for those of us who live in

urban areas. They are not needed for survival, and they act only as status symbols. Inhumane practices abound, including leaving animals such as the red fox, the lynx, the leopard and the ocelot with legs caught in steel-jawed traps that have been condemned world-wide as a cruel and primitive means of capturing them. Many species are becoming extinct, but until we oppose the fur trade they will continue to be captured. The only creature that has the right to own a real fur coat is the animal itself.

Make your own clothes

Be creative and make your own clothes. If you have access to a sewing machine, the time and some patterns, you can save money, become more self-reliant and dress more individually.

Read the labels

Reading the labels on your food isn't good enough. You must read the labels on your clothes too. Look out for mixes of natural and synthetic fibres and washing or cleaning instructions (does the garment need to be dry-cleaned or hand-washed?). Select clothes that will cut down on energy, expenditure on chemicals and specialist cleaners and, of course, pollution.

Buy alternative silk

China has been the world's largest silk producer for over 4,000 years, and the use of the mulberry silkmoth has become more intensive and mechanized. Fifty moths can deposit more than 20,000 eggs, which produce their silk in just three weeks. The pupa is killed in boiling water, acid or by gassing which keeps the cocoons intact and ensures the fine yarn of consistent strength that is needed for modern power looms. Hand-reeled raw silk is uneven and unsuitable for power looms, and the threads are drawn from cocoons softened in hot water. Alternatives to silk include alginate fibres from seaweed, ardil from peanuts and vicara from maize.

Polish your shoes

Shoe polish helps to keep your shoes in good condition, so that they will last longer than just a few moments in the rain. Keep your shoes in good condition in a non-toxic way. Tests in the USA have found seven toxic ingredients in ordinary shoe polish, including methylene chloride and nitrobenzene. Methylene chloride (also known as dichloromethane) is a known cancer-causing agent in animals and a strong skin irritant in humans. Buy non-toxic shoe cleaners that contain organic waxes, plant oils and pigments that aren't tested on animals, and help to reduce the number of needless chemicals that we produce.

Re-use your clothing

If you don't feel that your old clothing is good enough to recycle in a charity shop, recycle them at home. Cut up worn towels into small squares for facecloths. Turn old sheets and shirts into polishers and dishcloths. I remove buttons, zips and belts and keep them in a tin for emergencies and for when I feel creative.

Health and Well-being

Campaign against the car

The effects of the car on our health are serious. Apart from vast quantities of sulphur dioxide, nitrogen dioxide and lead, about 4,520,000 tonnes of carbon monoxide are released every year in Britain, hindering oxygen transport from the blood in the body tissues. Pregnant women and small children are especially at risk. World Health Organization limits for carbon monoxide emissions have been breached in London since 1987. The 740,000 tonnes of nitrogen oxides and 545,000 tonnes of hydrocarbons released into the environment every year from cars form ozone in sunlight. As the ozone levels in the environment increase, so do hospital admissions for heart diseases. Campaign against the car for better health. Use public transport, cycle or find other alternatives.

Protect yourself from DIY materials

In the race to save money and energy, many people are using potentially harmful materials in home-insulation applications. If you have to use mineral wool insulation, for example, the British Government advises that you should exercise extreme care, wear a mask and thick rubber gloves and never expose your skin to the material. You should put the mask in the dustbin when you have finished the task, wash all clothing and throw away any spare insulation material, in a separate bag, immediately. Keep loft hatches closed to prevent particles from blowing into the house. These warnings should be taken seriously by everyone. The business of saving energy is important, but your own health is also vital.

Don't use a douche or vaginal deodorant

Female douches generally contain ammonia, detergents, artificial fragrances and phenol, which is easily absorbed by the skin and is very toxic. So-called 'feminine hygiene sprays' are, of course, aerosols with artificial chemicals in them. Regular washing should keep you clean without these unnecessary products. If you have vaginal smells or discharges that worry you, it is far better to see a doctor than to try to cover up the smell. Try bathing with a few drops of tea tree and lavender oil.

Learn to love a tree

Trees stand proud as the most magnificent and the oldest of all plantlife on this planet. Some alternative health specialists actually recommend hugging trees to get energized. Five minutes sitting under an oak can make you feel serene and calm. Why not learn to love a tree?

Clean wounds with clean spirits

Some medical disinfectants – indeed, some of the best-known – contain trichlorophenol, a mixture of chlorinated phenols that are known to be corrosive and dangerous. One and a half grams of phenol have caused death, and it is known to be poisonous through skin absorption. Rinsing a minor wound with soap and hot water, salt water or calendula lotion is adequate to kill bacteria; serious wounds should be treated in hospital.

Get rid of a sore throat with greens

I once had a cut on the roof of my mouth. I spent two weeks using chemical mouthwashes and antiseptics to no avail, when a friend told me I was being too harsh on myself. She suggested gargling or drinking boiled sage tea. It worked so well that I have recommended it for sore throats, tonsils, spots and cuts, and it has never let me down. It tastes *awful*, so to get a child to drink it I recommend adding a little honey. Cut down on the chemicals in your bathroom cabinet, and get some sage.

Plant trees in hospital grounds

There is some evidence that patients in hospitals have a faster rate of recovery if they can see trees from their windows. Local conservation groups should work together with hospitals to create an atmosphere of beauty and peace around hospital grounds. Orchards will be especially beneficial, offering not only trees but also their fruit, and may even provide a form of therapy for patients who are well enough to help look after them.

Stick up for wild chimps

Animal experiments for medical research are a controversial issue. Many pills and cures have been tested on animals to check safety and reactions before being given to humans. There is an important argument against these experiments, however. West African chimpanzees are increasingly under threat because they are being exported for medical research. Chimps have blood groups that are similar to those found in humans and are therefore very valuable for such research. The World Wide Fund for Nature estimates that 34 per cent of the primate species are vulnerable. However great our need for cures, we cannot condemn other primates to possible extinction in order to cure ourselves. Not all experiments can be justified as necessary to save human lives. Chimps have been electrocuted, starved, beaten, frozen, burned, blinded and killed, often without painkillers, for causes that are at best ridiculous and at worst barbaric.

Don't support drugs and animal experiments

In 1984, at the University of Texas, kittens were injected with the hallucinogenic drug LSD to study their behaviour. The kittens became uncoordinated and displayed reactions that included vomiting and body spasms. We do not need to inject animals with such drugs to determine reactions that may be different to humans' in any case.

Cut down on drugs

There are 18,000 licensed medicines on the British market, yet the World Health Organization tells us that only 200 drugs and vaccines are absolutely necessary. Only one-third of all prescriptions are prepared and taken properly. The pharmaceutical industry tries to get us to buy more and more drugs, not just to make us better but so it can make profit. Our lifestyle, the food we eat and the stress our bodies suffer are largely preventable. Think carefully before you take tablets. Are they really necessary, or is there another way of solving your problem?

Don't eat more than you need

One of the greatest tragedies of so-called 'developed' societies is that our affluence is literally killing us. A diet high in animal fat, cholesterol-rich dairy foods, excessive intakes of sugar and refined processed food means that we suffer from heart attacks, obesity and high blood pressure. It is one of the major causes of death in Britain. By eating less and better food you will enjoy a healthier life and help the planet by cutting down on waste, over-refined foods and packaging.

Reject animal testing to find cancer cures

One of the medical profession's best myths is that we must test drugs on animals to find a cure for that terrible disease, cancer. The World Health Organization says that 80 per cent of cancers are related to lifestyle and environmental factors and are, therefore, largely preventable. Industrial chemicals, smoking, food additives and bad diets are all known causes. After fifty years of experiments on animals, scientists have found that other methods of research are more cost-effective, more humane and more accurate. Clinical research on humans was the method used for the first major breakthrough for the drugs used in chemotherapy treatment. Ten rare cancers can now be cured with drugs developed by human studies. The National Cancer Institute has tested 'cures' on 500,000 animals to date, with a success rate of only 0.0001 per cent. This slaughter cannot be justified. Support cancer charities that do not use animals, like the Macmillan Cancer Relief Foundation and Quest for a Test for Cancer. Ask others to stop experimenting on animals.

Look after yourself

Look after yourself. Take care of your own health and you will have the energy to care for others. If you really want to save the planet, start by saving yourself first: no one else is as interested! Get enough sleep; eat a good diet; reduce your stress levels; do not expose yourself to unnecessary chemicals; and keep fit.

Think deep ecology

In the rainforests of Australia groups of people met to discuss their despair over the state of the planet. They were frightened, angry and confused. Everything around them seemed to be in a state of collapse, and the forest they wanted to save was soon to be destroyed for hardwood logging. In 1984, as a result of this meeting came the Council of All Beings, a unique consolation for those who feel despondent about the monumental task ahead. Many people feel that we are inseparable from nature, but few of us have the chance to enjoy an imtimate relationship with it and to gain strength from the contact. Deep ecology aims to help us remember our connection with the planet, reassess our lives and help us find clarity, inspiration and commitment.

Eat less beef

Growing numbers of cattle are providing the planet with an unusual problem – they belch and break wind, giving off methane, a potent greenhouse gas. Methane accounts for 18 per cent of the greenhouse effect. And that is not all. It takes more than twenty times the energy you get from your steak to feed the animal in the first place. This means that huge amounts of grain and soya, which could be used as a staple diet for millions of people, are grown to feed cattle.

Get rid of your own headache

Nine out of ten headaches are the result of stress, including anxiety, depression, worry and other emotional problems. American Food and Drug investigators have concluded that tablets provide no relief for this type of headache. They recommend taking tablets only for a fever or a hangover. For natural headache relief, drink a herb tea like chamomile, mint or rosemary, get a massage, relax your neck, try to cut down the stress and get some sleep. Sit quietly, upright and with your feet firmly on the ground, and imagine energy coming away from the head. These simple measures could save a great deal of the £1,500 million we spend in Britain every year on drugs and free resources for research into more acute illness.

Support population planning

Women's powerlessness, the degradation of the environment, social inadequacies and hunger are the main causes of the population problems this planet now faces. For depressed countries the only source of power for the poor is children. The single most important step to be taken by First World countries is to give women the world over the power to plan their families. International policy has to change. The answer is not just to dish out drugs or injections but to share our wealth and our knowledge with everyone.

Balance your diet

An average American consumes 2 kilograms (4.4 lb) of food every day, but Belgium was given the honour of being the leading calorie-consuming nation in 1989 with an average daily consumption of 3,850 calories. We can enjoy a delicious and nutritious diet without eating to excess. Saving this planet is about saving people too.

Overcome your addictions

Large fertile areas of land are devoted to feeding the addictions of a few, mostly in the industrialized world, with cigarettes, heroin, sugar, coffee and alcohol. Help is available from groups such as Alcoholics Anonymous, but awareness of the causes and consequences of addiction, in oneself and in others, is essential. We need to share responsibility globally for the damage done to the environment and our life chances by addictions.

Don't use tampons

Tampons have been surrounded by controversy since the early 1980s, when it was discovered that there was a direct link between Toxic Shock Syndrome (TSS) and tampon use in the USA. But as long ago as 1942 doctors expressed concern about their use, and more recently studies have found that up to 75 per cent of women using tampons have encountered problems. Tampons also do environmental damage. The cotton is produced only with the help of pesticides, and the rayon, derived from wood pulp, is manufactured using chlorine, which forms dioxins as by-products and pollutes the rivers and seas. Tampons are not sterilized: The Women's Environmental Network exposed the industry during 1989 with the publication of 'The Sanitary Protection Scandal'. Use sanitary pads instead.

Find out about allergies

The heavily polluted environment of today is directly responsible for an increase in allergies and similar illnesses. Allergies can cause asthma (which can kill), eczema, hyperactivity, hayfever, colics, etc. Humankind has become allergic to a number of foods and products because of sensitivity to chemicals. Dr Jean Munro from the Allergy and Environment department at Nightingale Hospital, London, has described the spread of intolerance to chemicals as 'epidemic'; our bodies are reacting to more and more chemical stimuli and coming under enormous stress. By reducing or eliminating food additives, atmospheric pollution, pesticides, water pollution and other chemical stimuli we can reduce the risk of allergies.

Use herbs for minor illnesses

Many of the illnesses that we suffer are minor: sore throats, spots, insect bites and headaches. There are numerous alternatives to the billions of tablets that we put down our mouths every day, and they have been around for centuries. Use natural cures for minor illnesses. Consult good alternative health books, and buy your herbs from reputable health food shops, but, above all, get to know your body and the causes of your discomfort. You will be able to help yourself get better with a positive attitude to your body.

Use homoeopathy

Homoeopathy works on the principle that like cures like. Homoeopathic remedies are made from herbs, salts, minerals and, in some cases, diseased tissue in minute dilutions. The potentized remedies (as the diluted medicines are called) are given to the patient to stimulate the individual's own healing process of the body, rather like vaccines. It is unwise to try to treat yourself for anything other than minor ailments, as the remedies are prescribed precisely for the individual, taking family history, likes and dislikes and emotions into account. Homoeopathy does work. I have had it myself, with excellent results. It could well be the medicine of the future, as it has little or no detrimental effect on the environment, offers a holistic attitude to patient care and has no history of animal experimentation.

Stimulate your senses the natural way

Use essential oils to stimulate and to cleanse. They offer an alternative to aerosol air fresheners and chemical bath oils, and they are good for massages. They are derived from aromatic plants and trees and smell wonderful if warmed over a candle to give a room an extra special atmosphere. Essential oils are widely available.

Try acupuncture

Acupuncture has been practised for over 3,000 years in the East. The basis of this healing art is that health is the balance between two opposing forces, Yin and Yang, and our body, in a state of constant flux between the two forces, becomes ill when they are no longer in harmony. Acupuncture rights the balance by stimulating points along lines of the body with fine needles, which conduct vital energy. It is known as a 'holistic' healing method; it considers stress and emotions along with physical illness, and it is said to be 60 per cent effective for chronic pain suffers. It involves no use of chemicals or drugs and has no adverse environmental effects.

Relax!

Stress and stress-related illnesses account for a large proportion of modern sickness. Meditation may help you relax. Join a class, or try sitting quietly at home and concentrating on your breathing for half an hour.

Try reusable incontinence pads

About one in four women suffer from incontinence at some time during their life, and in the last few years companies have been marketing disposable paper incontinence pads, which are generally bulky and expensive. Their environmental effects range from pollution at the paper mill, in the form of dioxins and furans when the paper is bleached, to disposal. The plastic backing is not biodegradable and, when wrapped up and put in the dustbin, will be around for about 500 years. Try using washable incontinence pads, which save money and offer more dignity than a bulky paper nappy.

Nose for problems

Every year we buy 310 million boxes of paper tissues in Britain. Bleached white tissue, which is impossible to recycle, is an unacceptable indulgence. If every person in the world used a box of tissues every month, there would be no trees left on the entire planet. Handkerchiefs originated in France in the fifteenth century, when sailors returned from the Orient with lightweight linen *couvrechefs* (coverings for the head). The anglicized word handkerchief was adopted when these cloths began to be carried in the hand. They then became a fashion item, and in 1530 they were recommended as nose wipers by Erasmus of Rotterdam. Cotton handkerchiefs are now widely available. As well as being cheaper in the long run, they are much less wasteful.

Stop smoking

Cigarettes are a hazard not only to your health but also to the environment. The poisons in cigarettes include heavy metals, dioxins and pesticide residues, and the trillions of cigarettes smoked around the world every year create pollution for everyone. Not only does the tobacco plant take minerals from the soil and require large amounts of pesticides, but also it is estimated that 12,000 square kilometres (4,800 square miles) of forest are needed to fuel tobacco-curing factories each year. Do not harm yourself and others with cigarettes.

Avoid unnecessary x-rays

By far and away the largest source of artifically created radiation that we expose ourselves to is x-rays. The risks may outweigh the benefits: it is estimated that they contribute to 1,500 extra cancers in Britain each year. Serious accident victims need x-rays, but you do not need them every time you visit the dentist or hospital, so take extra care to be protected and agree to x-rays only if they are vital. If you do need an x-ray insist on a lead shield to protect your organs.

Save the rhino

The rhino is seriously threatened with extinction. It has been hunted for over 1,000 years, and in 1987 there were only a few thousand of the species left. It is literally being hunted to death by man because of an ancient superstition that rhino horn has great magical and medicinal powers. Poaching gangs are sophisticated and well paid, often causing havoc in national parks and game reserves. Within fifteen years the rhino will be extinct unless we demand firm international action. Don't buy this type of 'medicine'.

Get rid of smog

One of the most upsetting things I learned early on as an environmentalist was that some of the nicest-looking sunsets are actually caused by the reaction of sunlight with chemical compounds that we have discharged into the atmosphere. These come from car pollution, factories and gases. They can be particularly poisonous to animals and affect our lungs. The British Lung Foundation suggested that Londoners should wear masks to protect them in 1989, when levels of pollutants were extremely high. Especially at risk were people who suffered from asthma or bronchial diseases and chest infections.

Use your car less and reduce your own use of chemicals, and you will help to eliminate smog.

Spread the word about pesticide poisoning

Doctors know very little about the treatment and diagnosis of pesticide-related illnesses, yet as many as 250,000 people worldwide may be affected. Farm workers are exposed to a potentially dangerous chemical cocktail of poisons used in our intensive agricultural system. Cases of mass poisoning have been reported all over the world. The public is at risk through ingestion of contaminated foodstuffs, especially unwashed fruit and vegetables. They are even at risk when walking in the countryside. The effects of pesticides range from cancers and diseases of the central nervous system to kidney failure, skin diseases and even memory loss. There is only a handful of specialist hospitals that understand the full effects of chemical poisoning by pesticides. Their possible effect on the next generation is not clear at all. Demand more research.

Reject the vitamin supplement

Herbal extracts, vitamin supplements, mineral tablets and other health supplements are a healthy business, but they may not have any effect on us. The industry is worth over £135 million a year in Britain. The public swallowed over 3,000 million tablets in 1987 alone. If you eat a generally good diet, you shouldn't need any of them. Most good diets produce more than enough of the minerals and vitamins that our bodies need. Only those who smoke cigarettes, don't eat properly and take other tablets are likely to need multi-vitamin tablets. Mineral supplements are unnecessary. We need only a few millionths of a gram of most elements, and they may be toxic to our bodies if taken in tablet form. Deficiencies are almost unknown in industrialized countries. Don't bother with supplements: check your diet.

Slow down naturally

The hectic and fast-moving lifestyle of the 1990s will bring with it problems that will take more than drugs to solve. Over 1 million people in Britain are said to be addicted to tranquillizers to help them cope with the stresses and strains of their unnatural environment. The Department of Health has urged that all tranquillizers should be prescribed for shorter periods and for fewer conditions. Alternative and holistic methods for calming your body down include relaxing massages, deep breathing and meditation, herbal teas, drinking less coffee, giving up additives and sugar and finding counsellors with whom to talk through your problems.

Walk it

Walking 1 mile every day can make you fitter and you could lose one pound of weight every week. No pollution, no fuss.

Protect the rainforests

There are about 3,000 plants with known cancer-curing properties, and about three-quarters of these grow in tropical rainforests. There may be many more. We may never know the true cost of the destruction of these precious ecosystems.

Say no to drugs

Doctors often give us medication in the form of drugs because they think we expect it, not because they know it will cure us. Cut down on the number of chemicals you accept into your body, and reduce the production of potentially harmful drugs.

Cut down on fluoride

Fluoride was considered a poison until Italian dentists in the early 1800s found that it helped to reduce cavities in the teeth, although its use often led to unsightly teeth. In the 1930s metal-refining industries found that they had to dispose of quantities of corrosive and dangerous fluoride, and they came up with the idea of selling it to water companies. The body can tolerate tiny amounts of fluoride without serious side-effects, although more than 4 milligrams per day can cause brittle teeth and abnormal bone formation. Reject fluoride in toothpaste, and campaign against it in water. You could get quite enough fluoride from tea, because of the soil it grows in, and from fresh vegetables.

Cut down on chlorine

Chlorine and its compounds occur in bleaches and disinfectants, household cleaners and fire extinguishers. It is used in processing wood pulp, in refining sugar, in manufacturing dyes, drugs and oils and in the preparation of frozen vegetables. Chlorine is extremely reactive. It links up with other chemicals and can form compounds that are extremely dangerous for the environment and for your health. Many people are sensitive to chlorine without realizing – notice your reaction in swimming pools, for instance? Cut out chlorinated bleaches and refined foodstuffs that use it, and campaign for chlorine-free paper.

Reduce your solvent intake

Many products contain solvents: polystyrene and plastic products, decaffeinated coffee, foods containing glycerol (such as ice-creams, cakes and biscuits), ink, lipstick, dyes, detergents and deodorants. Some are more toxic than others, but together they represent a considerable daily exposure, and their continued manufacture poisons our environment. Look for nontoxic alternatives.

Breathe!

Most people don't breathe properly. We use only part of our lungs to keep us alive. Breathing properly will massage every organ in your body. This will do more for your health and well-being than a handful of assorted tablets and pills, and it's free. Take time off every day, practise breathing at bus stops, on the train, while you wash-up – very soon it will be second nature.

Check your dentist

Some people who have had fillings removed find that they feel more alert and think more clearly and that their memory improves. The fillings contain mercury, silver, copper, tin and sometimes zinc. Chewing releases small amounts of filling into the food in your mouth and over a long period of time may poison you. In 1987 the Swedish Government banned the use of mercury fillings in the teeth of pregnant women because of the risks to the foetus. It saw the ban as the first step in its programme to phase out the use of mercury in dentistry. Mercury fillings in teeth can affect the immune system. Ask your dentist to use an alternative compound.

Laugh

Don't take the world too seriously. Laughter can help lighten the load – laughing relaxes your whole body, deepens breathing, expands blood vessels, improves circulation and speeds tissue healing. We may not be able to solve all our problems with laughter, but we can certainly make the world a more pleasant place to live in.

Talk about it

Don't bottle up your misery. Talking your problems through with a friend, a counsellor or a member of the family could be a lifesaver. A good listener will help to solve some of your worries immediately and will guide you on the road to healthy confidence and self-esteem.

Death

Start a 'Trees for Remembrance' scheme

When loved ones die they can leave behind a future for tomorrow. Plant trees as life and death celebrations that will serve too as living monuments that everyone can enjoy.

Ash is no fertilizer

Scattering the cremated remains of a body around a rose bush or flowers won't help them to grow. It might even kill them. Disperse the ash over as wide an area as possible, or ask the crematorium to dispose of the remains for you.

Choose sustainable coffins

At least 80 per cent of the 600,000 coffins used in Britain every year are made from chipboard and veneer, imported from Belgium. Most of the veneer comes from tropical rainforest sources, and the chipboard itself is bonded with pollutant formaldehyde glues and resins. The remaining 20 per cent of coffins are made of oak from North America. To make an environmentally sound choice we should stop importing tropical hardwood veneers such as the 2,000 cubic metres (2,600 cubic yards) that came from Belgium during 1988 and campaign against the use of formaldehyde, which is a suspected human carcinogen and irritant. Buy North American oak or British woods if you can.

• *Avoid PVC*

Polyvinyl chloride (PVC) linings for coffins are causing an environmental problem. Crematoria in Britain have Crown immunity for pollution emissions, and concern has been expressed about the high levels of dioxins measured around them. Dioxins were found in ash from one crematorium in Wales. No likely source for these could be found until it was discovered that PVC was used for coffin linings. These create dioxins when burnt. Alternatives exist; make sure that they are used instead of PVC.

Young Greens

Children and Young People

Use your head

Children can quite easily pick up nits or lice from other children at school. If your child has become infested, the first thing you're likely to do is to rush down to the chemist. But the chemical mixtures in head-lice shampoos include lindane, carbaryl and malathion, which are pesticides. Lindane is the most dangerous and was banned as an ingredient in sheep-dip some years ago. Try getting rid of the lice using non-toxic alternatives such as cider or malt vinegar, or the oils of rosemary, eucalyptus, geranium, lavender or coconut. Rub the oil into your child's scalp and then use a steel comb to remove the dead lice. Applying natural oils is not only a much safer but a cheaper remedy too.

Don't let young children play near busy roads and motorways

Children like the sense of thrill and adventure associated with fast cars but, playing by the roadside, they are often oblivious to the very real dangers involved. Quite apart from the obvious risk of an extremely serious or even fatal accident, there are also some invisible threats. Brain disease, asthma, colic, palsy and anaemia are illnesses that may be triggered by exposure to the fumes of leaded petrol and other exhaust gases emitted by cars.

Reject disposable nappies

The British disposable-nappy market is worth over £330 million each year. But this convenient product has enormous environmental implications. For a start, one average-sized tree must be felled to produce between 500 and 1,000 nappies. Until the advent of the Women's Environmental Network's campaign in 1989, after which changes were introduced, the paper pulp used was chlorine-bleached, causing problems with dioxin contamination. The use of a mixture of plastics and synthetic absorbancy chemicals is still part of the production process. In short, the cost – economic and environmental – of using and disposing of these nappies is enormous: they make up roughly 4 per cent of our household waste; and studies from the USA have shown that they take over 500 years to biodegrade. So, save yourself money and help the environment. Use recyclable cloth nappies instead whenever you can.

Use a nappy service

Nappy services are on the increase in North America and have many advantages. They are good news for your baby, who gets clean, comfortable cotton nappies; less energy is expended as the nappies are washed collectively; and, because the nappies are non-disposable, this means no plastics and chemicals and saves trees. Using a nappy service also works out cheaper than stocking up on disposables. What's more, you no longer have to wash nappies yourself: they get collected each week and swapped for bright, clean sterilized ones.

Give greener rewards

It is difficult enough being a parent, but knowing whether to give sweets as a reward for good behaviour to small children can be a real dilemma. Sugar aggravates tooth decay, and giving your children sweets, chocolate bars, fizzy drinks and biscuits is, as far as the body is concerned, a punishment, not a reward. So, isn't the risk to your child's health, on the one hand, and the cost of unnecessary, expensive packaging on the other, rather a high price to pay for the few minutes of relief you get from the pacified child chewing on a sweet reward?

Serve them 'real' snacks

Why not serve your children 'real' food from an early age? Cut up fruit and vegetables – oranges, apples, carrots, etc. – into bite-size chunks for snacks for young children and offer them raisins and nuts when they get older.

Wean them off baby-foods

Baby-food with labels marked 'sugar-free' or 'low sugar' can still contain up to 25 per cent pure sugar, according to the British Maternity Alliance. Government recommendations that the amount of sugar in baby-foods should be reduced have only encouraged manufacturers to seek out alternatives, which they do not disclose, such as glucose, artificial sweeteners and fructose. Baby-food should be entirely sugar-free and, until companies agree to use correct labelling, you should avoid them. If you prepare babies' food from the natural foodstuffs you eat yourself, their diet will be far healthier *and* cheaper.

Breast is very much the best

Breast-feeding is the best option for the environmentally conscious mother, as well as the safest for the baby. For every 3 million mothers who bottle-feed their babies, over 70,000 tonnes of waste tinplate are produced from discarded packaging. Multi-nationals selling bottle formula for feeding babies can't reproduce the exact ingredients of breast milk, even with additives. Yet despite the benefits, in Western countries the biggest disincentive to breast-feeding is having to contend with the embarrassed reactions or downright insensitivity of many people, including doctors and health officials. If you want to breast-feed and are at all concerned about it, contact support groups before you have your baby.

Avoid using a personal stereo

Early in 1990 the National Deaf Children's Society tested all the personal stereos on the market in Britain and found that every single one of them was capable of an output of 90 decibels, the equivalent to the noise of a pneumatic drill. This is particularly dangerous for children's ears as sounds entering are condensed into a much smaller and more delicate ear canal. Furthermore, the sounds are refined to a much higher pitch, so the level of pressure in the ear is greater. A vicious circle then ensues: listening to over-loud music impairs our ability to detect higher frequencies (the ones we use to 'listen' to music with), so we have to turn the noise up in order to hear it. Apart from being potentially dangerous to the individuals using them, personal stereos also cause noise 'pollution' for other people. All told, this alienating 'toy' can be more of a hazard than it seems.

Buy them green toys

Hamleys in London, the biggest toyshop in the world, have reported that environmentally conscious consumers are beginning to turn away from the gadget-type toy to more traditional, well-built items like wooden dolls and teddy bears. This trend implies an enormous saving of resources in the long run, with a reduction in the numbers of broken, gimmicky toys, their batteries all run down, that children discard so quickly after Christmas and birthdays. By contrast, well-made teddy bears can last for generations and indeed have recently risen to the status of collector's items.

Get them to make things

Instead of mass-produced toys, why not encourage your child to use a bit of imagination? They can make things from boxes, empty containers, scraps of cloth, beads, and natural things. You'll save money and lose your sense of dismay at seeing children taking expensive toys apart. This approach can also help to cut down on some of the wasteful packaging of young children's toys.

Hair is good for the garden

Use children's hair clippings on your garden. The nitrogen in hair can release itself over many years, feeding trees or shrubs.

Try pre-natal care

Looking after yourself before you have a child is as important as what happens to your body during pregnancy. A healthy baby, conceived in a healthy body, has a higher chance of survival and of better health in its lifetime. The water that we drink, the food that we eat and the air that we breathe all have an effect on our bodies. If you think you want to start a family, get some advice about pre-natal care.

Give your child a massage

Children need and love to be touched. A soothing, relaxing massage will help to calm them down at night and get a good night's sleep. I prefer to use almond oil with tiny drops of different essential oils for different moods. Massage helps children who are anxious or depressed and can even calm hyperactive children. It also encourages bonding between parents and children. Tell them that you love them.

Avoid hazardous chemicals

Pregnancy brings with it some risks and changes in your life. Many pregnant mothers cut down on tobacco and alcohol or other drugs, but some hidden chemicals may have acute effects on pregnant women. In the USA doctors advise women against using cleaning products, hair dyes, food additives and perfumes, even tea and coffee. (The aware green person would do well to avoid these anyway.)

Cut down on ultrasound scans

The World Health Organization has questioned the use of scanning by high-frequency sound waves to monitor a foetus in the womb. There seem to be no long-term safety studies on this technology, but reports from the USA have claimed a link between scanning and hearing disorders; some have linked scans with dyslexia. Many mothers have said that their children appeared to be affected by the scan and tried to move away in the womb. Until we know more about the long-term implications of scans, a pregnant mother might question their use if they aren't vital.

Don't have x-rays if you are pregnant

X-rays and pregnancy don't mix. In the last thirty years we've realized that routine x-rays for pregnant mothers have been responsible for cases of leukaemia and other long-term cancers in children. It is now known that any exposure to radiation from an x-ray can have an effect on the foetus, and children of any age should avoid x-rays except in emergencies.

Avoid 'disposable' babies

Millions of packets of disposable cloths, face and bottom wipes and cleaners are used on newborn babies each week. Manufacturers promote their advantages: they are quick and easy to use and they are disposable. They do contain fewer chemicals than throw-away wipes for adults, but they are made from products like wood pulp in the main and are pollutants.

*

Let your baby go bare!

Babies' bottoms are covered with plastics, disposable nappies and all manner of chemicals and creams. Nappy rash was virtually unheard of until plastic pants were introduced. Knitted wool covers offer some protection for babies when treated with lanolin and also allow the bottom to breathe, but the best idea is to let your baby go bare as often as possible, for as long as possible.

Don't let your child smoke

Passive smokers (those of us who do not actually smoke cigarettes but have to breathe in other people's smoke) are likely to suffer from illnesses such as catarrh, coughs, asthma and colds. Cadmium and lead from cigarettes can be absorbed by children whose parents smoke, and reports suggest that children are more irritable when they inhale nicotine. We know that a foetus is affected if its mother smokes during pregnancy. Why don't we accept that cigarettes have some effect on small children? For your children's sake, don't smoke.

Beware what you feed your child

Food is fun, but not the synthetic kind. Desserts, sweets, jellies and creams made with preservatives, colourings, emulsifiers and sugars are mostly junk. They can aggravate allergies, cause hyperactivity and increase the likelihood of other illnesses in children. Reject them.

Let them grow

Children love to grow things. It helps them to learn about nature and the world they live in. Encourage them to grow seeds, pips and bulbs at home. Grow fast-shooting sprouts and encourage them to eat them. They will quickly appreciate the link between what we eat and the soil.

Watch for intolerance to chemicals

A growing number of children are finding that they are allergic to milk and milk-based products, sugars and synthetic foods. Some doctors have been slow to recognize the symptoms; you, the parent, will be the best judge, so take note of what's wrong with your child, and take action where necessary.

Recycle clothes

Is it really worth spending huge amounts of money on clothes for children and small babies that will be worn for only a few months? Many thrift shops and charities sell practically brand-new baby clothes at a fraction of the cost. Recycle baby clothes, and teach your child to think green at the youngest possible age.

Let them read green

Hundreds of books for children illustrate the wonders of nature, explain pollution and explore ecology. Children's storybooks should be written in non-sexist, non-racist language, helping to develop their understanding of the world in a genuinely balanced way. If you are buying books for children, look for those that espouse good ecological and social principles.

Buy non-toxic toys

Toys with non-toxic ingredients, including paints and varnishes, are now available. Although lead has been removed from some paints, it and other harmful chemicals may be hidden in painted products. Don't buy your children toys unless you know that they are safe. Look for durable, hand-crafted toys. Don't buy those from rainforest hardwood sources, and reduce plastics, batteries and metals to a minimum. Teach your children to reject wasteful consumerism at an early age.

T.V. —
light radiation
sessions for all
the family —

Don't let children sit too near the television

Non-ionizing and electromagnetic radiation from television sets is still under scrutiny. The only thing that scientists agree on is that children shouldn't sit right in front of the television, as the radiation seems to be strongest there, though it quickly dissipates after 2 metres (6 feet). In Sweden manufacturers have come up with a model that cuts the radiation by half. Lobby for low-radiation models world-wide.

School and College

Raise funds for good environmental projects

Sponsoring positive environmental schemes abroad and at home is an excellent way for students and pupils to raise money and learn in the process. There are thousands of tree protection and planting schemes, seed schools, water-purifying projects and small solar schemes to promote.

Twin with an ecology-conscious school abroad

By twinning with a similarly ecology-conscious school or college you could swap notes on local environmental problems and successes and educate yourself about the world at the same time.

Plan a nature garden

You can learn so much about nature and wildlife from just a small patch of land: select plants for size and colour, learn about seasons, extend original habitats and create new ones for birds and butterflies, and grow herbs for food. A worthwhile venture will need the continuous involvement of teachers and parents and rotas for maintenance and watering.

Adopt a tree for lunch-time

Schools in Australia have been pioneering a new lunch-time exercise. Children 'adopt' a tree, and throughout their school or college life they eat under it, rest under it and care for it.

Go for violence-free science

During 1986 over 750,000 animals died in experiments in schools, universities and polytechnics. Students and campaigners are urging a ban on this cruel method of teaching. They are encouraging the study of science without animal abuse, and they are campaigning against any disciplinary or administrative action that could constrain students who wish to reject experimentation on animals.

Campaign for vegetarian school meals

Get your school to provide a range of alternative vegetarian meals at lunch-time. Lobby your local authority; get up a petition; get teachers on your side; ask your parents to write letters on your behalf; and send in sample menus that exclude meat dishes.

Ban additives from schools

A study by New York City's state schools during the first part of the 1980s concluded that children who eat fewer additives and chemicals are brighter and less aggressive. Over 1 million children took part in the study, and it was found that the average increase in academic ranking was 15 per cent among children who were served meals that were healthy and additive-free. For some children the only decent meal each day is the school lunch; local education authorities should be especially vigilant that tomorrow's generation has the best possible food.

Write and paint

Education about the environment isn't gained from textbooks alone. Share your concern about the plight of our planet by expressing your views in essays, stories and poems or by painting and drawing. Use your school magazine as a vehicle for disseminating information and stirring consciousness.

Negotiate a noise agreement

Noise is a polluter; it should be recognized as an environmental problem. Left unchecked, it can result in deafness in extreme cases. Caring for our bodies must include caring for our ears, and learning about the pollution from noise is an important beginning. Negotiate a noise agreement with your parents, school and neighbours, and keep everyone happy.

Test the pollution levels

Science labs are good places to start learning about pollution, and the environment around your school building is the place to begin. Test for acid rain, for instance, or do a survey on the amount of litter in the local area. Work out how much it would cost, in terms of money and energy, to put things right.

Campaign for better public transport

Most young people at school or college travel by public transport. Walking used to be fairly safe, but more and more accidents are taking place as roads are widened and schools are amalgamated to save money. Campaign for public transport that is safe and more friendly to the environment.

Use solar-powered calculators

If you use a calculator, reject batteries, which use fifty times more energy to produce than they actually provide – use a solar-powered calculator instead. They are the same price and never need renewing. They work even without direct sunlight; light from bulbs is enough to power them.

Make fast food a no-no

Fast food in the form of hamburgers, chips and hot dogs should be unacceptable to young people, who deserve a good diet. Peer pressure is the fastest way to stop the rot; green students will know of the problems associated with fast foods, which contain preservatives, colours, artificial ingredients and large amounts of fat and sugar – and are covered with wasteful packaging. Tell the others.

Plant a tree for each new class

Each year a new class of students arrives at every school and college. What better way to celebrate their arrival and be positive about the environment than to plant a tree for them? Perhaps the outgoing class could plant the tree for the incoming one? If there isn't space in the school grounds, ask the local authority or parks department to allow you to have a small piece of land.

Learn about Third World aid and development

The predicament of the so-called developing countries is a cause for concern around the world. Students should know that the lifestyle of the First World is responsible for chronic problems of the Third World – not to make them feel guilty but to empower them with information and to change their attitudes, so that tomorrow's generation will understand that we all share the natural resources of this planet and are responsible for preserving them.

Bring back the fountain pen

Throw-away pens have become the norm in schools, colleges and universities. We throw away literally millions of them. While no one wants to go back to the chalk-and-slate era, refillable ink pens will cost less and use up fewer resources.

Invite speakers to share their knowledge

Why not invite speakers from environmental or animal groups to tell you their story? They will help to widen the environmental debate and will supply information. Welcome speakers from industry and the Government too.

Make schools and colleges no-smoking zones

Most smoking starts in schools. Pressure from friends encourages many young people to start smoking and get hooked for no reason other than to keep up with their friends, who probably don't like it much either. The biggest contribution you can make to your health at school is to persuade everyone that smoking is socially unacceptable.

Attend cycling proficiency classes

Avoid accidents on the road: learn to cycle properly. After all, a car driver has to pass a test to get a licence. The least you can do is learn to ride a bicycle safely and well.

Check your computer

Now that many schools and colleges use computers for mathematics, computer studies and even languages, the issue of low-level radiation from computers is an important one. Sensible chairs, adequate ventilation and appropriate lighting are crucial; VDUs should be checked for radiation emission; and exposure should last for no more than an hour at a time. Good working practices should start at school, so that they carry on into adult working life.

Collect rubbish to save money

The collection of cans and scrap teaches young people to be aware of recycling and the dangers of litter but can also help obtain much needed income for school facilities. Negotiate a good price for the goods you collect. If people are prepared to offer decent clothes or bric-à-brac for collection, hold a jumble sale.

Put up a list

Pin up a highly visible list of environmental groups and charities, local and national, including local recycling centres and facilities, so that people will be able to contact their favourite groups.

Organize quizzes and competitions

Quizzes and competitions sharpen the brain. Why not hold

an environmental quiz and test the knowledge of the greenie smart-alecs?

Campaign for the return of the washable cloth

In washrooms and toilets across the country washable cotton cloths are being replaced by paper towels. These are energy-intensive: campaign for the return of the cotton cloth. Campaign for toilet paper that is made from recycled paper and chlorine-free.

Organize environmental days out

Days out are few and far between at schools, but they represent an important part of the year's curriculum: pupils learn more, faster, when a day out is involved. Whatever the reason for the next day out, why not extend the experience by asking to visit a local nature park, a windmill or an energy-saving centre?

Write to manufacturers

You will have to learn how to write cogent letters anyway, so why not start flexing your consumer muscles by writing to manufacturers and companies that produce environmentally unsafe products, asking them to change their ways? Learn how to argue persuasively by writing letters of complaint.

Check the tuck shop

The tuck shop may be the provider of many over-sugared, additive-laden sweets and snacks that are destroying your teeth as well as pouring chemicals and waste into your system. Ask for quality snacks, fresh fruit, mixed nuts and raisins to be added to the tuck-shop list. What about carob as an alternative

to chocolate, or freshly squeezed orange juice instead of the
sugared variety? What about sugar-free sweets?

Ban aerosols

Ban aerosols from your school or college, even ozone-friendly
ones. Don't forget that substitutes for CFCs in aerosols are
also either ozone-depleting or hydrocarbons, contributing to
the greenhouse effect. The safest environmental option is to
ban them all.

Have save-a-scrap days

Collect scrap materials such as egg boxes, unusual clothes,
containers for washing-up liquids and the like for primary
and pre-school groups, which love making things with them.
Scrap can be useful when it is transformed into material for
make-believe.

Sign petitions

Get involved. Collect and sign petitions on environmental
issues, and voice your protest with others.

Grow plants and flowers

Don't just grow a pip in a bottle: be adventurous and make
your school or college grounds something to be proud of.
Plant native flowers and vegetables. You can sell them and
cuttings at fêtes or jumbles to raise cash.

Make videos of local wildlife

Many schools and colleges offer access to video or photography equipment. If you have the chance to use it, you

could present a valuable record of local wildlife for generations to come as well as having fun learning.

Debate the issues

If your school or college hasn't already got one, start a debating society. A debating society will help you learn to articulate your concerns about this planet.

Do an environmental-impact study on your school or college

You could learn how to assess environmental impact by starting with the building in which you learn. An environmental-impact study could look at the waste you create, the amount of energy that is consumed there and even the effect of the equipment you use both on the local environment and from the moment that it is created until it is disposed of.

Form a group

Get together with a few friends and start an environment group. Discuss possible actions, meetings and campaigns, and teach each other. Join up with organizations that run youth groups, like Friends of the Earth.

Use only recycled paper

Campaign to get your school or college to use only recycled paper in the building. Some school notebooks are already made from recycled paper, but the number could be increased dramatically.

Collect paper

Collect notebooks from students when they have finished

with them, and add them to a paper collection in the school or college grounds.

Get environmental studies on to the core curriculum

Many schools and colleges now offer environmental studies but not as a core subject, which means that the subject is not compulsory. Ask for environmental studies as a core subject, so that proper exams will heighten young people's awareness of the planet.

Campaign for a green library section

Your college or school could set aside a special green section that contains books, magazines and newspapers about the environment.

Experiment with care

Chemistry laboratories should have a policy of recycling, or safely disposing of, all chemicals instead of pouring them indiscriminately down the drain to add to water pollution. There are regulations that govern the disposal of chemicals in schools. Are your science teachers observing them?

The Green Consumer

Shopping

Reject 'biodegradable' plastic

The plastics industry has begun to fight environmental criticisms of its products by introducing so-called 'biodegradable' plastics. These new starch-based plastics are expected to degrade into carbon dioxide and water when buried in wet soil. The green shopper should not be conned by these marketing promises as some of the 'biodegradable' plastics are only broken down into pieces so tiny that the human eye can no longer see them; these are called 'biodestructable' plastics. To replace small plastic polymers with starch ones literally means taking food from the hungry to appease your conscience. It is also unlikely that these plastics will degrade quickly in landfill sites. Plastics should be recycled and not left in rubbish tips to biodegrade. Biodegradable plastic takes more energy to produce, is not as durable as ordinary plastic and has less chance of being re-used.

Consider if you really need to go shopping

Shopping is said to be one of our favourite pastimes. During the consumer-boom in the 1980s we heard of the compulsive shopper, the professional shopper and the functional shopper. In the United States $3,191,353,425 is spent every day on shopping, and a proportion of that is for food and clothing that will never be eaten or worn. We waste food, chemicals and money spent on transportation and raw materials in this

way. The next time you feel like shopping, ask yourself if
you really need to go. If you do want to go window
shopping, try leaving your cheque book, money and credit
cards at home.

Buy in bulk

Buying goods in bulk does not only save you money, it also
saves on packaging, transportation and storage and it cuts
down on trips to the shops. Try finding a good cooperative
that buys vegetables and grains in bulk or buy fresh food
when you visit the countryside.

Read the label

You should get into the habit of reading the labels on your
foodstuffs. Find out what the E numbers mean; not all of
them are dangerous. Check for added salt and sugar which
you may want to avoid. All canned fruits and vegetables I
inspected in one major store contained sugar. Look for food
that has been produced without artificial chemicals or additives. Find out about the country of origin; you may want
to boycott the produce of particular countries.

Buy simple

With so many thousands of products to choose from on our
supermarket shelves, the average shopper can be forgiven
for being confused and buying too much. When shopping,
you will have to come to some decisions about the environmental problems facing you and buy only what you need.
To help cut down on pollution, buy products that have
been processed as little as possible and have travelled the
least distance.

Get out of the throw-away trap

You know that when you buy good quality, durable products they may cost more but will save you money as time goes on. It also helps the environment in many different ways by cutting down on the raw materials, packaging and processing of cheap mass-market goods, reducing pollution and billions of tonnes of waste. Always complain to manufacturers and shops who do not provide good, durable products.

Go without the carton

Cartons of milk and soft drinks may save energy in transportation as they can be stacked to take less room than, say, glass bottles. But the carton is not re-usable, recyclable or biodegradable. It is made from layers of highly bleached paper, aluminium and plastic which poison and pollute the environment from their processing until the end of the carton's non-re-usable life. We should be pressing for a better environmental alternative such as the re-usable glass bottle.

Shop at cooperatives

Shop within a cooperative and you will be supporting good businesses and small-scale manufacturing processes which are good for the planet. One of the most famous consumer cooperatives is the Japanese Seikatsu Club. It has 150,000 member households and is run and organized predominantly by women. The Club sells household products without adding profit and the fair price paid by the buyer is passed on to the farmer or producer. The cooperative does not need mass advertising but informs its members through a regular newsletter. Only one product in each line which meets strict environmental and health criteria is chosen. Cooperatives offer products based on sharing and need rather than profit and greed.

Buy recyclable packaging

The way your food is packaged is crucial to environmental considerations. Paper packaging that also contains strips of aluminium and plastic and styrofoam containers are impossible to recycle. Simple packaging of single layers of paper, steel, aluminium, glass and rubber is recyclable, but it is not worth buying if you simply throw it in the bin afterwards.

Do not buy goods packaged in more than two layers

There are virtually no products on the market that need more than two layers of packaging. Take a box of chocolates, for example. It can contain more packaging than actual sweets. Beauty products, gifts, games and sweets are the main over-packaged products. Most of the money you pay goes into the extra layers of packaging.

Refuse the plastic carrier-bag

Next time you go shopping, take your own carrier-bags or tough and durable shopping bags. Billions of plastic bags, none of which are recyclable or biodegradable, are given free to shoppers everywhere. There is a simple, green alternative: refuse and re-use.

Don't buy polystyrene packaging

Reject polystyrene packaging which contains chlorofluoro-carbons (CFCs) and damages the ozone layer. If the package is not labelled, then assume it does contain CFCs. Even the new packaging contains HCFC-22, or hydrocarbons that are called 'soft' greenhouse gases. Buy loose food, take your own bags or use recycled brown paper bags.

Write letters

The pen is mightier than the sword, they say, so why not use it? Write to packaging manufacturers and ask them to forgo CFCs and excess packaging on items you buy regularly. Write to manufacturers of tinned goods and ask them to remove the sugar. Write to paper suppliers and ask them to produce unbleached and recycled paper. Manufacturers will have to take notice as you are the customer and they will not have a market if you do not buy their goods. Get information and statistics to back up your request; always be polite and ask for a reply.

Don't be fooled by the freebie

Petrol stations give us toasters and fancy glasses. Cosmetic companies offer expensive towels and accessories. High-profit margins and fierce competition have made it worth their while, but many companies are now beginning to regret the trend, as customers seem to be more interested in the free gifts than in the products themselves. Don't be fooled by the free gift; ask yourself if you really need the product offered.

Buy from shops that have environmental policies

As consumers become more aware, many supermarkets and shops are now considering environmental policies. Choose your goods from shops that have stated policies for their own-label produce and that also require high standards from others. Honest and informative advertising and labelling are the fastest ways of ensuring you are well informed enough to make a choice. Ask for these; they are your right as a customer.

Support the small shop

Out-of-town hypermarkets and shopping malls with huge car parks have pushed the small, local shop to virtual bankruptcy. Small shops save on energy: you don't have to drive; you just walk there with a shopping bag. The shops are more likely to offer local produce and they provide a vital lifeline to people without cars.

Buy a rechargeable battery

If you must have a battery-powered product, then you should buy rechargeable batteries whenever possible. You can recycle them up to 500 times using a cheap battery charger. Although they save money and resources, rechargeables do contain cadmium, a highly toxic material, which is gradually being phased out of battery manufacture in Europe. One-third of the planet's cadmium goes into batteries, and the environmental effects are extremely serious. It is likely that manufacturers will come up with a safer rechargeable battery in the future, and we should encourage them to do so.

Ask for labels on fresh foods

Labelling has become important to today's shopper, but mostly for pre-packaged foodstuffs. Ask for labels to tell you about the pesticides that have been sprayed on unpackaged foods and also for information on how to wash off or get rid of unwanted residues. This action could spur more producers into dropping their use of some pesticides and you, the consumer, will be better informed.

Shop for an end to oppressive regimes

We often feel that we can't do very much when we see on television and in our newspapers pictures representing some

of the barbaric and oppressive regimes that operate throughout the world. The human suffering caused by the apartheid
regime in South Africa has made many of us aware of racism
and of our own political strength when it comes to boycotts.
When you shop, you can show that you care by not buying
products from countries with oppressive regimes.

Go to jumble sales

Pick up cheap secondhand goods. It's a form of recycling!

Buy a rainforest

Well, not really. You can support some rainforest groups that
buy 'protection' for rainforests. They should not be anyone's
to own, but protecting the rainforests means that indigenous
people can carry on living there and that the area will not be
developed by industry or cattle grazers. Organizations like
the World Wide Fund for Nature operate such schemes.

Beware the green label rip-off

Surveys by the British Consumers Association have pin-
pointed a new rip-off in the marketing world: the environmentally friendly product. Companies make excessive claims
about products like aerosol cans that are 'green' and batteries
that are 'environmentally friendly' because they have with-
drawn the mercury and cadmium content. My view is to
avoid products with the 'environmentally friendly' label. It
usually means that there is one good thing about them, but
potentially many other things are wrong. Companies that
produce truly 'friendly' goods do not need to say so quite as
boldly: their ingredients label and the information on the
packet should tell you everything.

Swap with friends

Swap clothes, goods you no longer need and other products with friends. Reinstate the art of re-using clothes and goods, save yourself money and have fun in the process.

Don't be fooled by advertising

Advertising products is big business. A company that can afford to advertise on television is usually promoting a highly manufactured and manipulated product. The cost is always passed on to you, the customer. Watch the adverts to judge the product for yourself. In North America 47 per cent of viewers find television adverts annoying and unnecessary.

Look out for planning controls

Supermarkets and hypermarkets are springing up everywhere. The land used is often just outside a town and large areas are concreted over. Before planning permission is granted, the plans have to be assessed and at this stage you can have an effect on the building. You may want to oppose it altogether or you may just want to get the developers to agree to certain conditions: for example, to keep the trees on the site.

Campaign for shopping crèches

Taking children shopping can be a hassle if they stop you from getting on with what you want to do. At supermarket checkouts sweets, chocolates, biscuits and crisps are stacked low on shelves to entice children. Shoppers' crèches could save you both stress and money. Campaign for a crèche in larger supermarkets and get smaller high-street shops to join together to provide them.

Give back the extra packaging

In Sweden toothpaste boxes will be phased out completely by the end of 1992 as this extra packaging is unnecessary and wastes energy and resources. When you next visit the supermarket, try leaving unnecessary packaging behind, or at least write to the manufacturers to complain about it. Someone will soon get the message.

Support the re-usable

Support companies that produce products and foods in re-usable containers like milk bottles, re-fillable plastic containers at the Body Shop, returnable soft drink bottles and packaging with a deposit to encourage you to bring it back.

Eating

Eat out at wholefood or vegetarian restaurants

Many restaurants are beginning to recognize the advantages of serving vegetarian and wholefood meals. My most rewarding meal in the United States was a visit to the legendary Moosewood Restaurant in Ithaca, New York State, a vegetarian restaurant that cannot be beaten. There are plenty of guides to other good wholefood restaurants around the world.

Cut down on chocolate

Britain leads the world in chocolate consumption. The number-one-selling sweet product is Kit Kat, followed closely by the Mars bar. Between them they generate sales worth £300 million a year. The British chocolate market alone is worth £2.4 billion each year. Cocoa, the main ingredient of chocolate, has come under the scrutiny of environmentalists recently because of the highly dangerous pesticides used on the cocoa bean. The chocolate bar itself is highly processed and sugared and this affects teeth, digestion and general health. Chocolate was favoured by the Quakers in the early eighteenth century as a healthy alternative to alcohol, but today's processed, pesticide-laden variety is hardly the same thing. Drink the purest cocoa you can find; eat chocolates sweetened with fructose (from pure fruits); and generally buy less chocolate.

Eat brown bread

As early as 1826 doctors warned of the health risks associated
with a diet based on white bread. White bread is highly
processed and robbed of much nutritional value. In the early
eighteenth century only the wealthy ate white bread, and
bakers would add lime, chalk and animal bones to make
bread whiter for the masses who wanted the same bread as
the wealthy. The plain reason for processing brown bread
into white is not to give you a better product, or even a
wider choice, but to cut the cost of baking and to make
higher profits using lots of air and water. Eat organic brown
bread whenever you can.

Eat real food

By buying pre-processed foods that are convenient and quick
you make yourself unhealthy as well as allowing the food-
processing industry to keep millions of the poor in developing
countries hungry. Lax controls, poor research, questionable
ethics, and the addition of chemicals and ingredients that are
known poisons are a real scandal. Most of us do not think
about the food we are eating. We take it for granted that
someone 'out there' will have our interests at heart (they
haven't always). But, as consumers, we have become addicted
to convenience food. We expect cheap, attractive-looking
food, packaged and clean, so food preparation does not
interrupt our lives. We could save so much energy and avoid
pollution if we started to choose food with a more discerning
eye. Over 75 per cent of the food North Americans eat is
processed in some way, and in energy terms, this costs over
$10 billion each year. Food processing adds directly to pollu-
tion, acid rain, the greenhouse effect and a host of other
environmental problems.

Buy fruit and vegetables in season

Buy fruit and vegetables in season and save energy on transportation, which in turn cuts down on pollution. We expect fruit such as bananas and oranges all year round. Many of the more exotic fruits are bought because they are on the shelf in front of us, transported thousands of miles out of season for us to eat. They are likely to have been treated with pesticides and chemicals to keep them fresher for longer. If you don't buy fruit and vegetables until they are in season, you will enjoy a better diet too. Every item of food that is grown and consumed locally is an important addition to your diet.

Boycott Faroe Islands fish

An all-out boycott of fish from the Faroe Islands was called for by environmentalists in 1989 after unsuccessful attempts to persuade the Faroese people to stop killing the pilot whale. The ritual slaughter of thousands of whales by the Faroese is not to provide subsistence food. The reason, groups like the Whale and Dolphin Conservation Society say, is sport. The whales are dragged to the shore with large hooks and incisions are made in their blowholes, causing a lingering death. The British and USA market take 90 per cent of Faroese fish.

Cut up your vegetables

If vegetables, meat and other foods are cut up as small as possible before cooking, you will find that they take half the time to cook and save energy and money as well. Potatoes for mashing can easily be cubed, for example, and carrots can be thinly sliced. Try cooking and steaming several vegetables together.

Boycott Californian grapes

The United Farmworkers Union in the USA has called for a boycott of Californian grapes because of the enormous suffering of workers using the pesticides: captan, methyl bromide and parathion. The 300,000 reported cases of poisoning per year do not even include the cancers and birth defects the workers and their families suffer. But the local environment suffers too, as groundwater contamination affects the local community and wildlife. Captan, one of the fungicides used, has been banned or severely restricted by Finland, Norway and Sweden, and even tiny amounts cause harm to fish.

Do without dried potato

The overpackaged 'space-age' dried potato is definitely not food for a greenie. Given its content of pyrophosphate, added vitamins, salt, dried whey, emulsifiers E471 and E450(a), preservatives E223, E220 and E222 and an anti-oxidant, E321, you could be forgiven for asking where the dried potato is! The energy you spend boiling an electric kettle to pour water on the dried version is comparable to the energy used to cook a potato on a gas cooker to mash yourself, so why not buy the real thing?

Reject irradiated food

Good fresh food does not need to be irradiated with cobalt-60 or caesium-137 to give it a longer shelf life. Environmental groups claim that food irradiation is just another way of using up nuclear waste, the irradiation source. Irradiation does not kill all the bacteria that are likely to be dangerous (for example, *Clostridium botulinum* is not affected and eating food contaminated with botulism can be fatal). Irradiation also affects foods in different ways, most notably in terms of flavour. It can reduce the flavour and vitamins in food and can destroy essential fatty acids. Some supermarkets have agreed not to sell irradiated food, so look out for them. If in doubt, ask before you buy.

Do without a beefburger

Tumble-massaged, stripped animal carcasses, gristle, sinew, heart, tongue and fat added to colourings, flavourings and preservatives – or just a beefburger? Most beefburgers will have come from farmed animals, intensively reared, that eat up to eight times their body weight in grains each year. Doing without beefburgers saves land and resources, and will give you a healthier diet too. Try a beanburger or another beef-free alternative.

Buy organic bread

Most supermarkets supply at least one kind of organic bread, and you can buy locally produced loaves from your health food shop. Over 10 million loaves are consumed in Britain every day: it's time we stood up for our staple food. The whole-grain wheat used for breadmaking is damaged by pesticide residues even before anything else is added to it. My local supermarket displays a notice on the bread shelf which reads: BREAD AND FLOUR PRODUCTS MAY CONTAIN ONE OR MORE OF THE FOLLOWING LISTED ADDITIVES: ANTIOXIDANT, ARTIFICIAL SWEETENER, COLOUR, FLAVOUR ENHANCER, FLA-VOURING PRESERVATIVE OR FLOUR IMPROVER. Obviously bread is not a simple product any more. In Britain the inclusion of vitamins and additives is required by law to replace some of those removed through processing. But whole-grain products, especially bran-based ones, have high pesticide residue levels – unless they are grown organically.

Campaign for real fruit

We buy fruit from supermarkets expecting it to be like boxes and tins, perfectly manufactured and without blemish, every piece tasting and looking like the others, with the same colour, texture and weight. Though there are 6,000 varieties of apple registered in Britain, only nine dominate our shops and markets. Fruit orchards used to be abundant; they offered not only apples, but also pears, cherries, plums, damsons and mulberries, with beautiful names like Cornish Honeypin,

Beurre d'Avalon and the Scarlet Crofton. Find out about local varieties and ask your grocer to name the varieties displayed. Buy organic, and shop around for 'real fruit' again.

Boycott yellowfin tuna

The yellowfin tuna congregate beneath schools of dolphins – primarily spotted and spinner dolphins but also striped and common dolphins – in the eastern tropical Pacific. Tuna fleets find their catch by following dolphins, then hauling them aboard or netting them in order to catch the tuna. Officially around 120,000 dolphins die in the eastern tropical Pacific each year, but the true figure may be nearer 250,000, severely depressing several dolphin populations. By boycotting yellowfin tuna you can say no to the companies who persist in destroying dolphins.

Forget frogs' legs

Bullfrogs are killed in Bangladesh and Indonesia for a range of food delicacies exported around the world. The legs are the only valuable part of the frog and the still living torsos often try to crawl away after their legs have been chopped off. Apart from the obvious cruelty involved in this trade, taking huge quantities of frogs from the wild has devastating environmental consequences. Frogs eat waterborne pests that destroy crops. When the Indian frog trade was at its height, India was earning £5.5 million each year by exporting frogs' legs, but spending £13 million on toxic pesticides to replace their natural pest controls. Ecological and humanitarian pressure encouraged the Indian Government to ban the export of frogs' legs. If you don't eat them, there will be no market for those exporting them today.

Don't eat veal

White veal was introduced to Britain from Holland, and it is one of the most extreme forms of factory farming. Within a few days of its birth, the calf is taken from its mother and put in a wooden crate 1.5 metres (5 feet) long and 56 centimetres (22 inches) wide. It remains there for fourteen weeks and is denied fibrous food. Instead, it is fed purely on a diet of liquid milk substitute. The calf is kept intentionally short of iron so that we can eat 'pure' white meat. This practice should be stopped immediately, and you should boycott veal completely. In Britain every year we eat the meat of about 100,000 calves that have been reared in this way.

Boycott abattoir-slaughtered venison

Eager to develop the venison industry, dealers are trying to get abattoir-slaughtered venison regularized in the same manner as cows, pigs and sheep. The most humane way to slaughter deer is for them to be shot on the farm by qualified marksmen.

Reject rennet

In order to turn milk into cheese, rennet, a gelling agent, is used. Most people do not realize that rennet is taken from the stomachs of slaughtered baby calves. Not all cheeses contain rennet, but you can be sure of avoiding it by buying cheese with the vegetarian symbol.

Go vegetarian

In Britain over 3 million people are now vegetarian, making a stand against factory farming, intensive rearing, artificial foodstuffs and hormones in animals. There is a large variety of foods to eat, so life as a vegetarian can be healthier and just as much fun.

Campaign to clean up slaughterhouses

Of the 1,000 slaughterhouses in Britain, 900 of them are so filthy that imports are forbidden by every country in the world. Contamination by flies and excrement (from sloppy slaughtering), and fatty machinery growing mould, proves that killing animals is a dirty business in more ways than one.

Buy real pork

Factory-farmed pigs live on concrete or slatted floors and lie in their own excrement. Breeding sows are often chained to the floor and the others are tied so tightly that they cannot take a step forwards or backwards. Piglets are born in a farrowing crate and the mother is only allowed to suckle for two or three weeks before the piglets are taken to battery cages to be fattened up for market. Some supermarkets have complained about these conditions and pigs are beginning to be better treated. We eat 15.5 million pigs in Britain alone each year. Ask your supermarket for information about the pork you intend to eat, or give it up altogether if you are not satisfied with their answers.

Check the Es

Not all E numbers are dangerous as some are made from natural ingredients and are permitted colourants and preservatives. Others are not quite as pleasant. Some, like amaranth (E123), are products of the petroleum industry and have been linked to causing hyperactivity in children. Amaranth has been banned in the USSR and USA. Many of the Es banned in North America are in widespread use in Britain until they are proved dangerous. A number of books and pamphlets are available, so check out the E numbers in your food.

Make your own ice-cream

Every summer the British public forks out £40 million for soft ice-creams, yet Britain leads Europe in producing a product without any cream in it at all. Soft ice-cream is made by mixing a powder containing concentrated skimmed milk with added fat, emulsifiers and stabilizers, and blended with sugar. The result is 40 per cent sugar, 30 per cent fat, 25 per cent non-fat milk solids and 2 per cent additives. The secret in soft ice-cream manufacture is to get as much air into it as possible. Instead of paying for sweet air, why not make your own ice-cream or choose one of the natural brands now available in supermarkets?

Beware of food poisoning.

In spite of modern technology, bacterial food-poisoning cases have increased by 62 per cent, according to the London Food Commission. Poisoning was often blamed on the customer for bad food handling, but the 20,000 reported cases in Britain in 1987 suggest that the food industry is responsible for dirty and unsafe practices. Hygiene and environmental standards down the whole food chain – in farms, abattoirs, factories, shops, supermarkets and restaurants – have to be improved. An independent Health Department, separate from agricultural and food producer interests, would be a good start.

Have a great salad

The average British lettuce has been tested and found to contain 10 milligrams of nitrates. Chlorothanonil and permethrin, probable carcinogens, have been found in tomatoes from the USA. Fifty different pesticides are used for onions and seventy-five for cucumbers, including dieldrin. The very symbol of health, the salad, has become a health hazard. Always wash salad ingredients carefully and peel everything possible. Otherwise grow your own or buy organic produce.

Reject the broiler chicken

Most broiler chickens are reared in semi-darkness in huge sheds with up to 100,000 other chickens. They are genetically manipulated to produce as much edible meat as possible. At seven weeks the chickens are slaughtered by stunning them with an electrical charge in a bath and then their throats are automatically slit. In Britain some 500 million chickens are killed this way every year, as are a further 30 million turkeys. Reject intensively reared chickens as there are alternatives.

Salt of the earth?

Salt has been used as a food preserver for centuries. Now with the introduction of the fridge and freezer it is used mostly for taste and we still eat more than ten times the amount our body actually needs. Salt is added to pre-processed foods – another good reason for giving *them* up. The habit of shaking the salt cellar over every meal is wasteful and possibly dangerous as too much salt in the body can cause heart conditions.

Eggs for whose health?

The eggs scandal unleashed in Britain by former Health Minister Edwina Currie in 1988 sent shockwaves throughout the industry. From an average consumption per person of 200 eggs every year, sales dropped to less than half this level and hundreds of thousands of hens had to be slaughtered. The real scandal centred around the bacteria and salmonella levels found in eggs. Hens were being fed ground up dead chickens and contaminated foodstuffs. The cruelty involved in battery-caged and intensively reared hens is encouraging more and more people to buy free-range eggs. In Switzerland a law was recently passed ensuring that all hens were to be free range: allowing them space to move around and to go outside – a luxury not afforded to battery-reared hens. Over 2 million battery hens die prematurely each year because of the conditions and the average battery hen lasts less than a year before its egg output starts to fall off and it is slaughtered. You can help directly by buying free-range eggs, cutting down on the number you buy and by searching for the still rare organic egg.

Cut down on sugar

The British are among the highest consumers of sugar in the world, devouring over 113 grams (4 oz) each day. The high level of consumption is blamed on the number of pre-packed foods that contain sugar – sometimes without the consumer being aware of it. Sugar causes tooth decay and is indirectly linked to the increase in obesity, diabetes, heart disease and even gallstones. Yet sugar is big business and even government officials do not always want to rock the boat when it comes to advising the public about health. A normal diet, especially with plenty of fruit, will give you enough fructose and sweetness without additional sugar.

You are what you eat

The average person in Britain eats over 4 kilograms (9 lb) of chemicals and additives every year. Add to that the residues of pesticides on our fresh foods and pollution from our tap water and from the air, and consider the amount of chemicals that could have a disastrous effect on us. Many of the pesticides that were once used are now considered dangerous, but with around 1 million new chemicals being invented every year it may be many years before we realize the full danger of our industrial lifestyle. Food is crucial to our well-being: eating organic, additive-free food will help our bodies as well as the environment.

An apple a day may not keep the doctor away

Publicity over the use of alar, the plant-growth regulator on apples, has prompted the withdrawal of the chemical by the manufacturer, Uniroyal. About 40 per cent of our apples were said to be treated. When apples are turned into apple juice or apple sauce, a by-product chemical, UDMH, is formed which many studies in the USA have shown to be a human carcinogen. Even though the British Government has so far refused to ban the chemical, the recent public outcry and the manufacturer's response has ensured that alar is no longer an unknown chemical. Other pesticides and growth regulators are used on the humble apple however, and tests have found traces of diphenylamine and captan. Captan is a possible human carcinogen and although the residues will be reduced by washing or cooking, I recommend you peel all non-organic apples before you eat them.

Buy cardboard egg cartons

Cardboard egg cartons are generally made from recycled paper which saves energy and resources, and cuts down pollution. Until fairly recently most British supermarkets used foam cartons. These were ozone destroyers as CFCs were used in their manufacture. But all over the world today manufacturers are switching to less damaging materials. Use recycled cardboard whenever you can.

Nature does not create perfect fruit

When you buy fresh fruit and vegetables you generally get those chosen and approved by the big supermarket chains or markets. The produce looks perfect in every way. Often individually wrapped or boxed and without a blemish on them, you could be forgiven for thinking that they are the fruits of paradise. But this marketing is causing problems all over the world. Our standards are so high that we end up wasting food, energy, packaging and chemicals. Do you really need every banana to be the same length, or your cucumbers to be straight? Natural vegetable moulds can be easily washed off. Try to live without chemicals. It will make a big difference and will help you to accept the so-called visual quality of the superior organic produce more easily.

Go without the individually wrapped snack

Every lunch-time we manage to consume millions of packets of crisps, small cartons of fruit drinks, biscuits and snacks. These mini-packs take far more energy and money to produce than standard packs – which is why you pay more for them – and, of course, they are thus far more damaging to the environment. Take your lunch with you or buy in bulk and save the rest for another day. Buy foods that are not heavily wrapped. Cut pollution and costs, and save trees.

Go without wax

Certain fruits and vegetables have been waxed before they get to you to keep the skin from shrivelling up and to make the product look more appetizing. If you do not eat the skin of oranges, cucumbers, grapefruits and avocados, you might not notice, but those of you who cook with lemon rind, for example, will be safer using the organic or unwaxed varieties.

The waxes are usually authorized to contain paraffin, synthetic resins, shellacs and fungicides like benomyl, orthophenyl-phenols, imazalil and dicloran. In the USA the Federal Food, Drug and Cosmetic Act is supposed to require all shops to label waxed products, but this does not seem to be a priority in many stores. Go without wax whenever you can.

Learn to love mushy tomatoes

Over a hundred pesticides can be used on tomatoes to keep greenfly and other insects at bay. But few companies have been able to beat the mushy tomato syndrome. Every year the average USA citizen buys about 11 kilograms (24 lb) of tomatoes and at least 0.9 kilogram (2 lb) are thrown away because they are squashed. Multinationals are working around the clock to engineer the perfect tomato, but we could accept battered and mushy tomatoes to make chutney and tomato sauce.

Campaign for organic strawberries

In the early 1980s Friends of the Earth UK organized a campaign against the use of pesticides in foods. They concen-trated on strawberries and ran an advert of a blue plastic box containing a dozen tantalizing-looking strawberries, asking: 'Which contains more chemicals, the strawberries or the box?' The fears about strawberries are real. When the Natural Resources Defence Council tested strawberries in the USA, they found more pesticide residues than in any other fruit or vegetable. The residue most commonly found in fresh straw-berries is captan, a possible human carcinogen. It can be reduced by cooking and washing, but the chemical itself, already banned or restricted in Finland, Norway and Sweden, is known to harm fish and other water life even in extremely small concentrations.

Check your cabbage

Cabbages are part of our staple diet in winter. The American Food and Drug Administration has registered over sixty types of pesticides used for cabbages, but the most commonly occurring ones are methamidophos, diethoate, fenvalerate and permethrin. Washing, removing the outer leaves, peeling and cooking will all help to reduce these residues. Many of the pesticides are possible human carcinogens, and careful washing is vital. Whenever possible, buy organically grown cabbage.

Recycle your margarine tubs

Margarine tubs and yoghurt pots are usually made from acrylonitrile butadiene styrene (ABS) or polypropylene, a type of plastic which is easily recyclable. Although the technology is available to recycle this type of plastic, for many billions of plastic margarine, coleslaw and dessert pots the only thing we can do at the moment is to use them constructively as extra food containers, seedling and plant pots or even as children's toys.

Buy Brazil nuts

Brazil nuts need a great deal of care to grow properly. They do come from Brazil, but the farmers who have traditionally cropped them are under threat from the destroyers of the rainforests. Brazil nuts can be grown only in a rainforest setting, as they need a unique mixture of wildlife and trees in order to flourish. There is also the serious risk from aflatoxin if the nuts are not stored correctly or eaten at their best, so eat fresh Brazil nuts to save the rainforests.

Think about food

The production of livestock for our tables costs more than the life of the animal. It takes 4.5 kilograms (10 lb) of grain to yield just 0.4 kilogram (1 lb) of intensively reared beef. It is not just a resource problem for during the Ethiopian famine we imported their cereal to feed our cattle. A diet based on soya protein could feed up to thirty times as many people as a meat-based diet. Four hectares (10 acres) of land will support sixty-one people on soya and only two people on beef. None the less, 15 million children die each year from starvation or disease from lack of food.

Do not throw away your chopsticks

Japan, the country that uses one-tenth of all the world's wood, throws away billions of pairs of chopsticks each year. When these were invented in China and the Far East many centuries ago they were family heirlooms that were often passed down from generation to generation. One family in the forests of Malaysia complained bitterly that their lives were being torn apart for the manufacture of chopsticks while they shared just one pair, crafted by their ancestors, between a whole family. These days Chinese and Japanese food is eaten around the world; it is usually much better for you than fast food, but avoid the throw-away chopstick.

Campaign against the plastic fishing-net

New fishing-nets made with plastics that are invisible to most birds are wreaking havoc on the marine environment. Sea birds, like the razorbill, guillemots and shags are being hauled in the nets in their thousands. Porpoises, dolphins, turtles and smaller fish are also caught as the trailing nets, sometimes over 3 kilometres (2 miles) long, are dragged along the sea collecting every live creature possible and wiping the sea clean. Japan may be responsible for the death of over 100,000 sea mammals each year. A few countries have banned the most dangerous nets but the majority of our fish comes from nets considered unsound by conservation groups. Ask about your fish before you buy it. Get your local supermarket or fishmonger to buy only from reputable fishing industries.

Go for a natural shade of pink

Farmed fish are fed synthetic food colouring to make their flesh turn a more expensive shade of pink. The colouring is canthaxanthin, better known as E161. But it isn't just trout and salmon that are coloured with this additive. Some preserves, pickles, fish fingers and chicken, as well as 'sun-tanning' tablets, use it. The British Food Advisory Committee recommends that canthaxanthin should be restricted to use in fish only. Because it is too expensive to feed farmed fish on their usual diet of shrimps, prawns and other shellfish, they are fed instead on canthaxanthin to make them an appetizing pink.

Cut down on tin cans

Most of our cat food, tinned vegetables, soup and other similar products come in a tin. There are very few recycling facilities for tin in Britain and North America even though large quantities of it are home produced. Tin is not only energy consuming, but heavy to transport and tin smelting plants have produced vast quantities of pollution. Try to buy fresh vegetables and cut down on the amount of non-essential tins you buy.

Try vegetarian pâté

Pâté de foie gras used to be the kingpin of pâtés – until we discovered how it was made, that is. It is produced exclusively from the livers of force-fed geese. Some reports say that the geese have their feet nailed to boards while they are forced to eat 2.5 kilograms (5.5 lb) of salted fatty maize a day. Yet left to feed themselves they can produce a pâté of better quality. Leave the geese alone and try a vegetarian pâté made from mushrooms, peppers and soya as an alternative.

Buy sea salt

Sea salt is dried in the sun and production takes half the energy it does to find rock salt from under the earth. I find I mostly use salt to cover over and soak up red wine stains on carpets and for when I need a good scourer in the kitchen, but I rarely eat it and food tastes much better without it. Salt has been linked to heart disease and the World Health Organization recommends only 5 grams (0.2 oz) per day. In Britain and the USA we consume at least double that figure.

Avoid gelatine

Gelatine is one of those insidious ingredients that crop up everywhere. It is found in jellies, sweets, biscuits, ready-made desserts and cakes – especially those with glazes. The leftover of animal gristle and bone make up the main ingredients, and you should always check the label for gelatine if you want to avoid animal products. Wholefood shops sell alternatives.

Eat healthier jam

Jams usually contain more sugar than fruit. Sugar was originally used to preserve the fruit so that it could be eaten all winter. Mrs Beeton wrote in 1859 that 'sugar overpowers and destroys the sub-acid taste so desirable in many fruits'. You can buy jams and preserves made from organic fruits without sugar, preservatives, colourings and chemicals and refrigerate them. However, they are so tasty they don't even last long in the fridge.

Eat more honey

Bees work hard to produce honey, a natural sweetener that is
better for us than refined sugars. If you can't give up sugar in
your hot drinks, try half a teaspoon of honey as an alternative.

Use organic olive oil

Olive oil, and especially organic olive oil, is probably the
purest form of cooking oil there is. It is recommended as the
best and safest to use for salads, frying and roasting. Sunflower
and pure nut oils come next as healthy options.

Don't buy rape seed

Rape seed has been taking over the British countryside. Over 350,000 hectares (875,000 acres) of land were cultivated in 1988. It is used in cheap vegetable cooking oils and as the main ingredient in many biscuits and sweets. The pollen seems to be able to travel huge distances, and as an imported crop rape might be difficult to control. Rape seed has been associated with the increasing number of serious hay fever and asthma cases in recent years and doctors have called for more studies.

Fight obesity

Obese people generally do not eat twelve organic apples to satisfy their hunger. They consume chocolate, sweets, crisps, cakes and all manner of sugars and carbohydrates. Those suffering from obesity may well be suffering from an illness making them eat more and more of this type of food. One theory is that obese people store up more chemical and pesticide residues in their fat and when they try to slim with conventional slimming aids, usually increasing their intake of chemicals, they get a toxic body-load too high for the liver, which can be damaged. Their body fights to reduce the toxic load to the liver by making the person crave more food. Chemicals and fat are an important issue for the 1990s and more research must be done. Food addiction self-help therapy is often a good way to come to terms with this problem.

Make your own crisps

The processing of fresh potato into dried crisps is a classic example of how food can be manipulated to cost more than it's worth. A packet of crisps needs energy, oils, fats, salts and sugars and ends up costing 500 times more than the original potato. Why not make your own crisps at home?

Learn to cook

It is not a joke. Many people just don't know how to cook and end up buying prepared meals with all the packaging, additives and problems that processed food brings with it. As we spend less time cooking today, many cookbooks have been written with fantastic quick recipes, so you do not have to spend hours in the kitchen. Read a cookbook and try out the recipes.

Buy wholefoods

Wholefoods are unrefined, simple foods. They are usually pulses, grains, nuts, fruits and vegetables that have not been processed and do not have additives or chemicals added. Less processing and refinement means that less energy is used in production and you get a healthier food. Wholefood shops sell many varieties of what used to be staple foods. Some supermarkets have reintroduced wholefoods and they work out much cheaper than processed foods.

Eat more raw food

Raw foods, especially fruits and vegetables, are better for your body and also for the environment as they use little or no energy in their preparation. Raw food loses none of the essential vitamins and minerals that are lost in overcooked vegetables, for instance. You should always buy raw food in preference to frozen, tinned or processed varieties. Buy organic, but if you cannot, wash everything thoroughly before eating it.

Sprout food for health

Sprouted foods are simple to grow and extremely nutritious. You only need a few jam jars, clean water and fresh seeds or pulses. The seeds give a volume of about eight times their weight and only take about three to five days to grow. Many raw energy recipe books give details of how to grow what works out to be an extremely cheap, nutritious food.

Make your own yoghurt

Yoghurt is important for our bodies because of the lactic acid bacteria it contains. It is simple and easy to make and you do not need the stabilizers and artificial sweeteners that are found in some shop-bought varieties. It is often naturally sweeter than plain shop-bought yoghurt and you do not need to go to a lot of trouble to make it.

Eat more nuts

Many nuts have more advantages than you might think. They are a simple food, low in the food chain and need no processing. This saves energy, pollution and waste. Pumpkin seeds could help people with bladder-related illnesses; sunflower seeds have vitamins A, B, D and E and are good for headaches; all nuts give protein and energy that outshine meat-protein foods, help cut down on heart disease and provide tasty snack alternatives to sweets.

Don't waste it

During 1987 over 2.5 million tonnes of vegetables and fruit were destroyed by the EEC because prices had to be maintained at certain levels. Butter mountains, wine lakes and tonnes of meats, vegetables and fruits rot while people starve because our political and financial system cannot cope. This waste is not only unnecessary but cruel and environmentally bad. Campaign for a better system and don't waste food.

Pay more for your food

If we paid just 1 per cent more for our exotic fruits, it would be possible to pass on 10 per cent to the producer – the poor in developing countries. Pay the right price for your food to the right people.

Counteract 'heavy' metals

By eating lots of certain types of foods with calcium, vitamin C and traces of zinc, you can help absorb and destroy 'heavy' metals which come into your body. Eating apples, carrots and similar fresh, raw foods also helps as they are high in pectin. Toxic metals like lead, copper, aluminium, silver and mercury are absorbed and taken into the body by a number of routes but mostly through contaminated food.

Don't buy your fruit from the street

Fruits and vegetables displayed on stalls in heavy traffic will have high levels of lead in them. Unwrapped or unpeelable fruits and vegetables will have the highest risk. Car exhaust fumes, general air pollution and other contaminants get into food if it is left on display all day in the open air.

Discard the outer layers of vegetables

Cabbages, sprouts, lettuces and similar vegetables will have pesticides and chemicals sprayed over them while they grow, but they will also have been subjected to further contamination and pollutants from the air. Remove the outer layers of these foods (they're good for composting) and wash vegetables very carefully before you cook them.

Don't cook with aluminium

Aluminium foil comes from mined bauxite, some of which is from destroyed rainforest areas. It is extremely energy intensive to produce, using nearly six tonnes of oil for every tonne of aluminium. Too much aluminium in the body has been linked to memory loss, senile dementia and Alzheimer's disease. Reduce your intake of aluminium by not using aluminium foil when cooking foods. Avoid foods already packaged in aluminium. Do not grill foods on foil or put foods like potatoes in the oven wrapped in foil. Use a skewer instead.

Cut down on processed meats

Cured meats, like sausages, bacon, pies and hams, can contain added nitrates. Pies and sausages often include the slaughterhouse products that are not allowed in uncooked meat products: the brains, feet, rectum, stomach, udders, testicles and other parts of the animal. They are simply labelled as 'offal'. Water is usually the most important ingredient in processed meats and complicated 'rules' allow manufacturers to add vast amounts without declaring it clearly on the wrapping. Cut down on processed meat products for your health until manufacturers label their products clearly.

Spread a little less

Believe it or not, using less butter, margarine and other fats on your bread, breakfast toast and food can help towards better health, as well as help the environment. Too much fat in your diet encourages the use of intensively reared livestock, especially cows. This takes its toll on the land, the animals themselves and, of course, on the food that is grown to feed them. By cutting down on fats you will be less at risk from heart disease and of circulation problems.

Drinking

Do not buy beer cans with plastic ringpulls

Next time you think of buying a pack of four or six beers with a plastic can holder, think again. The ringpulls are said to take 400 years to biodegrade, and, left as litter, they create problems for wildlife on land and sea. They throttle birds that forage near dump sites, and animals like weasels or otters can choke to death on them. Around the coast sea mammals and dipping birds have had their lives shortened by this handy little device. If you stop buying them, the brewers will have to stop producing them.

Don't drink and drive

Never drink alcohol and drive. Numerous campaigns have been run by the British Government and by local and national action groups to stop this foolish and dangerous activity. Over 5,500 people die every year on British roads, and many more are very seriously injured. Drink-driving causes a large number of these deaths. In Australia the introduction of random breath-testing lowered drink-related accidents by one-third. European countries have followed suit, and in the USA Mothers Against Drinking and Driving forced many states to ban open drinks in cars and set up road blocks to catch drunk drivers.

Refuse hormones in drink products

During 1989 a row erupted over the sale of milk that was treated with the hormone bovine somatotrophin (BST), a hormone that can increase a cow's milk yield by up to 20 per cent. The long-term effects of hormone treatment on cows are still unknown, but in nearly every case tested so far the evidence has come down against their use. What is worse is that while testing has been taking place the milk has passed, unlabelled, into the general supply. Contact your milk supplier and complain. Refuse milk products containing BST.

Opt for chlorine-free cartons

Most fruit juices and over 20 per cent of milk in Britain are sold in cartons made of paper mixed with bleached paper, foil and polythene. Chlorine bleaches are used to make the paper white, causing serious environmental problems at paper mills when the waste is flushed away. Even more worrying are studies conducted by the Canadian and New Zealand Governments showing that dioxins, the chemical by-products of the paper bleaching process, are found in the paper and can migrate into the milk or juice itself. Some companies are now producing chlorine-free cartons, which are brown, but you will be better off using bottles and recycling them.

Try real cider

Cider is a traditional British drink, brewed originally from thousands of varieties of apples. Today many ciders are made from apple concentrate imported from countries that place few restrictions on chemical fertilization. The Alar pesticide scandal of 1989 pointed to real worries about the use of such chemicals on apples, as they may well be cancer-causing. Alar has been banned in the United States, but the British Government had given it the all-clear. Traditional cider and perry are made without chemicals, so look for them and support them whenever you can.

Use loose tea

The great British 'cuppa' is known all over the world, but nowadays we have created another use for paper in that convenient device, the tea bag. Millions of tonnes of chemically bleached pulp are mixed with wet-strength resins, including urea formaldehyde, to make tea bags. Tests have found dioxins, including the most dangerous, TCDD, in measurable quantities. Whenever possible, save paper; save on chemicals; and buy loose tea.

Don't drink yourself to death

Alcohol can be a killer. It destroys the liver and kidneys and the central nervous system, and it affects almost every faculty imaginable, from intellect to sight. Thousands of people are killed and injured on the roads each year as a consequence of alcohol-related driving accidents; thousands more die from related illnesses; and families have been emotionally destroyed by alcoholism. Alcohol can be addictive and should be treated as a drug at all times. It is to be enjoyed in moderation and should be produced without chemical interference or animal testing.

Try a herbal tea

Herbal teas are usually made from locally grown plants and are a delicious alternative to caffeine-laden coffee. There are now wonderful teas on the market, such as strawberry, chamomile and peppermint, some of which have medicinal properties too. Avoid those that are heavily overpackaged, and if your favourite is, write to the manufacturer about it. The best option is, of course, to make tea from your own herbs.

Tea is a treat

Tea is the favourite British drink. We manage to consume, on average, 1,355 cups per year per person. (North Americans, on the other hand, drink only 154 cups per person.) It is generally thought to be a good drink for you and the environment. There are few chemical additives, preservatives or sweeteners, unless you add them yourself in the form of milk and sugar. Tea plantations have a bad reputation when it comes to paying reasonable salaries to their workers, though. We think of tea as a cheap drink. If it were not so cheap, we would think twice about throwing it down the sink so readily. Why not buy your tea from cooperatives that ensure that some of the profits go to the workers?

Reduce your caffeine intake

The amount of caffeine in coffee is much higher than in tea, but coffee is fast becoming the number-one hot drink in affluent countries. Environmental problems are caused chiefly by the pesticides used on the coffee plantations. Caffeine has been linked with high blood pressure and heart diseases; doctors recommend cutting down on your caffeine intake. If you can find organic coffee, buy it, but try to reduce the amount of coffee you drink.

Re-use your coffee filters

Although some of the big coffee-filter manufacturers have been quick to produce chlorine-free coffee filters after the Women's Environmental Network protested about the environmental problems caused by bleaching them white, we do not need to use expensive paper filters at all. Rinse out a metallic or cotton re-usable filter.

Reduce your milk and milk-product intake

Milk and milk-based products are Britain's number-one food items. But milk is one of the most sensitive and allergenic foodstuffs. The majority of the world's population does not drink milk or eat milk-based products at all, and those people manage to get all the nutrients and calcium they need to survive. The intensive rearing of cattle for milk production uses valuable land, and the cattle eat much of what could give us an alternative source of protein and calcium. Milk has been implicated in over 70 per cent of cases of allergic skin reaction and nearly 90 per cent of asthma cases. If you have breathing or sinus difficulties, try giving up milk completely and you will notice the difference. Use milk as a special additional food and not as a staple food, and you will be in better health. You will also reduce the need for intensive cattle rearing.

Oppose animal abuse when testing alcohol

Animals are literally forced to be inebriated to test the effect that alcohol has on humans. During 1987, 3,746 animals were 'tested' with alcohol. There can be no justification for this cruelty.

Recycle your PET

PET bottles have become a household wonder. They are lighter than ordinary glass bottles and, if accidentally dropped, they will not smash, which saves on wastage. PET stands for polyethylene terephthalate, and no data exist to suggest its toxicity. We do know that these bottles are not biodegradable, though they can be recycled. As there are few facilities for recycling the billions of PET bottles produced, we should send them back to manufacturers and ask them to recycle the bottles until they can establish specific collection points.

Recycle your can

We buy a staggering 13.5 billion cans every year in Britain, 5 billion for soft drinks and the rest for foods, paints and pet foods. Aluminium cans can now be recycled in many areas, and in the next few years we should see the small number of cans we recycle rise to a more environmentally acceptable level. When you buy your next canned drink, remember that over 80 per cent of the cost is for the can itself! Avoid buying things in cans; recycle the cans; and opt for draught or bottled drinks (as long as you aim to recycle your bottles too). Recycling cans saves up to 95 per cent of the energy cost of producing them.

Drink safer water

The water that comes from our taps these days may be far from safe. It may contain nitrates, lead, aluminium, pesticide, fertilizer residues and a host of other chemicals, some of which are natural. Chlorine, used in water-treatment plants to

kill bacteria, forms trihalomethanes if mixed with organic
material such as peat from moorland or lowland rivers. These
are thought to cause cancer of the bowel and bladder, and
new studies have linked increases in leukaemia with chlorinated drinking water. Until we can all have safer drinking
water it may be best to filter your water, using approved

filters. The only goal we should have, however, is safer, cleaner water to drink from our taps.

Bottled chemicals

A bottle of mineral water may not be a safer product. Tests of many bottled waters have identified bacteria, pesticides and nitrates. Add to this the environmental cost of producing non-returnable, non-biodegradable, plastic and glass bottles. Fizzy mineral water is a good alternative to alcohol and if you buy a clear glass bottle it can at least be recycled, but beware – there are no approved standards for the production of such water yet.

Choose organic and animal-free wines

Organic wines are on the increase as discerning drinkers are rejecting wines treated with sorbic acid, sulphur dioxide, ammonium sulphate, diammonium phosphate and up to fourteen applications of pesticides. Animal and mineral extracts are used in the production of wine, including edible gelatine from bones, isinglass from the bladders of fish, casein and potassium caseinate from milk, albumin from egg, dried blood powder, tannin from wood, kaolin and clays. Many organic wine growers claim that you will not get a hangover if you drink organic.

Brave a better beer

Beer used to be made from four simple ingredients: hops, malt, yeast and water. These days we have no way of knowing what exactly is in our beer, and the biggest chemical ingredient, ammonia caramel (E150), is prepared by the controlled heat treatment of carbohydrates with ammonia. This is not considered to be toxic, but vegetarians or vegans will want to avoid beers that have been force-fed to animals for testing and those that use isinglass finings, which come from the bladders of fish. Buy beers that have been filtered without using animals. Animal rights groups can supply lists.

Do not buy paper or plastic cups

The waxed paper cup was invented in 1907 by an American, Hugh Moore. He produced it to sell pure chilled drinking water, and it soon replaced the communal drinking 'sipper' as a symbol of good health. The idea took off, and now everything from water to ice-cream is sold in it. Each year we use billions of disposable paper cups around the world as our parties and celebrations have moved away from glasses to throw-away paper or plastics. The paper cup comes from paper bleached with chlorine, which inevitably causes dioxin contamination around the paper mills, leading in turn to pollution of the water system. Plastic cups are made from petrochemicals, and they too have their own environmental impact. Use strong glass wherever you can.

Go for 100 per cent juice

Fruit drinks are not always what they seem. Most juice drinks that we buy contain as little as 15 per cent fruit, and they usually cost as much as the real thing. Some contain colourings, flavourings and large amounts of disguised sugars and artificial sweeteners. Go for 100 per cent juice whenever you can. Try squeezing an orange (in its own biodegradable wrapper) and you'll be sure of getting the real thing. Campaign for better labelling.

Complain about your drinking water

The tap water that millions of Britons are drinking may not meet the European Community's legally binding standards. Write a letter to the people in charge of tap-water quality in your area. By law you are entitled to ask for details of contaminants in samples exceeding the legal limits and to make a formal complaint to the water authority, the Government and the European Parliament.

Presents and Parties

Don't fly away with balloons

Balloons are used by campaigners and party-goers alike, yet most of us are not aware of the environmental problems they may cause. If they end up in the ocean, for example, they may kill the fauna that swallow them. Sea-turtles are at particular risk, as once a balloon has lost its colour, it looks just like jellyfish, their favourite food; but the larger sea-creatures are also threatened. In 1985 a 17-foot-long female sperm whale died of starvation off the New Jersey coast because the balloon she had ingested blocked the valve connecting her stomach to her intestine. Foil balloons are not biodegradable. Rubber balloons are, but they have clips and strings that also cause problems. They all must be disposed of carefully.

Buy a potted Christmas tree

Your Christmas tree dies the minute it is chopped from its roots, but if you buy a locally grown tree in a tub, with its roots, you may replant it in your garden after the festive season. Millions of trees could be spared in this way. However, a real green alternative is to decorate the large house-plants in your home.

Buy green books as presents

There are now many green books on the market and some,

like this one, are printed on recycled paper. With hundreds of titles to choose from, you will be able to select valuable and informative gifts for everyone.

Golden problems

One of our most precious metals, gold, is bought and sold all over the world. It is central to the functioning of our financial institutions, and its price has changed little over the years. Much of the gold on the world market comes from South Africa and the USSR, but gold can also be found in the forests of the Amazon. Gold processing uses and produces cyanide and mercury, which are responsible for water pollution and particularly toxic to fish and aquatic life. In South Africa bad working conditions, pollution and poverty shorten the lives of many of the black gold miners and the Anti-Apartheid Movement has called for the boycott of South African gold. In Brazil, where there are 50,000 gold diggers, gold mining is destroying the fabric of the Amazonian rainforests and putting the lives of the Yanomami people at risk. Think carefully before you buy your next gold present.

Wrap up presents with something different

Instead of wrapping your presents in paper that has been

bleached, why not think of something a bit more unusual? Recycled paper in natural colours, banana paper, hessian, muslin, rush or bracken, wool or cotton are alternatives that make presents look really special.

Do not buy ivory

There are only 600,000 elephants left in Africa. In 1979 there were 1.5 million. Elephants are killed by poachers using either dynamite or bullets to provide us with exotic ivory trinkets, carvings and piano keys. Their tusks are bought whole by Japan, Hong Kong and Taiwan and, after being cut, are sold around the world. Sustained campaigning by groups like the Environmental Investigations Agency has brought about a moratorium on the ivory trade that should be strictly enforced. Do not buy ivory presents, wherever you are. Boycotting the market in such trinkets will help to protect one of our most majestic mammals.

Do not buy kangaroo gifts

The Australian Government allows the killing of 2 million kangaroos every year. It says that their number needs to be kept down and that useful products can be made from their skin and meat. Millions of dollars are made around the world out of the sale of kangaroo-hair toys, kangaroo-skin car-seat covers, gloves and rugs, and kangaroo meat is used in pet food. If we stop buying such items, we may find that the kangaroos do not need to be shot at all.

Be careful with fireworks

Fireworks can be fun for humans, but they are terrifying for animals. The RSPCA advises cat and dog owners to give sedatives to nervous pets when fireworks are to be let off near them. The chemicals in the fireworks are not only a danger to people but their production constitutes an environmental hazard. You could have just as much fun baking potatoes and chestnuts on an open fire with friends.

Serve organic food at parties

If you cannot afford fresh organic fruit and vegetables all year round, or find them difficult to get hold of, serve them as a special treat at Christmas and birthday parties and on other special occasions.

Save the crocodile

Every year 340,000 crocodiles are killed for their skins out of which expensive shoes, handbags and briefcases are made. Only a few farms exist, so most crocodiles are captured in the wild in Papua New Guinea, Venezuela and India, and in the Nile and the Pacific. The crocodile-skin trade is worth $68 million: one average skin is worth $200. The biggest markets are Japan and France, but other countries import crocodile skins too. Do not buy items made out of the skin of wild animals like the crocodile.

Boycott battery-operated presents

Buying presents at Christmas and for birthdays is difficult; there is always a huge selection of new and exciting games and products available. One way of helping to protect the environment is to stop buying battery-operated toys. The energy spent making a battery is fifty times greater than the energy you will ever get from it – a waste of resources on non-essential goods. The batteries themselves contain toxic and dangerous substances, including cadmium and mercury which may leak if the batteries become damp. Even 'greener' batteries may contain zinc, carbon, mercuric chloride and alkaline manganese.

Don't forget the walrus

Now that concern over the mass culling of elephants is increasing, the next mammal on the hit list for tusks is the walrus. Greenland and Canada have access to walrus tusks: the only way to make their sale unacceptable is to boycott it and to campaign to stop the trade now.

Support local flower growers

Flowers make lovely presents to receive and give: greener flowers are even nicer! Those imported from other countries are more likely to have been sprayed with pesticides than those bought from small-scale local growers, and they have also been flown from overseas at great expense and energy. Also bear in mind that recent concern has been voiced over the health conditions of women in Honduras who earn their living growing carnations to send to Britain. So if you have a garden, grow your own flowers; if you don't, start asking about chemical-free alternatives.

Always serve non-alcoholic drinks

Do not encourage drunk driving; at your parties always have a choice of interesting and tasty alcohol-free drinks. You can make a hot apple punch without alcohol and serve exotic fruit bowls, shakes and juices. Non-alcoholic wine has a nice flavour and, as non-alcoholic beer is the biggest growth area in the brewing market, there are now plenty of brands to choose from.

Recycle your Christmas tree

On 6 January every year 35 million Christmas trees are thrown away as rubbish in the USA. But these days new schemes are emerging whereby, for the cost of $1, you can recycle your tree: it is chipped and made into a mulch that is then either sold or spread in public parks. Some communities in Texas have been using the trees as a base for dunes to fight beach erosion, which saves them from being dumped in overflowing rubbish tips.

Organize a green raffle

Raffles, sales and prizes in national and local events play an important role in the community. You could start to influence any committee, organization, church or group that you belong to next time you decide on a raffle as a fund-raising idea. Why not have green prizes? Reject the car, chemical products, the rainforest-wood furniture. Go for organic hampers, bikes, ramblers' holidays, cruelty-free cosmetics and recycled paper kits.

Greening your hampers

Hampers have always been exciting presents to receive. These days you can put together a more than acceptable green hamper that includes organic wines and champagnes, organic fruit and vegetables and even sugar-free alternatives to sweets and desserts. Add some real holly and a hamper basket from your favourite charity shop, and you have a very special gift.

Free-range it at Christmas

Christmas and Thanksgiving are traditional occasions for serving turkey. In Britain 36 million turkeys are scoffed each year, 98 per cent of which are factory-farmed. Free-range and organically reared turkeys are the choice for the green meat-eater. They cost more, but the meat is apparently more succulent and tastier.

Investment

Choose your home carefully

The purchase of a new home, of whatever size, will probably be the biggest expenditure the average person ever makes. You should consider it as a long-term investment. If the house you are planning to buy is being built, you may be in a position to insist that the builders include energy efficiency and even the use of non-toxic materials in the specification. Many of the larger building companies are beginning to sell green houses. Don't be conned into paying too high a price, however. Some companies, like Ferguson's in Northern Ireland, have been building energy-efficient houses for years at no extra cost to the buyer, so shop around and choose your home carefully.

Ethical friendly unit trusts

If you have over £1,000 to invest and you want to buy unit trusts, there are some that operate according to strict principles that are based not just on environmental considerations but on a range of tenets that the average 'green' would endorse. You can avoid businesses associated with the arms trade, alcohol, gambling and animal exploitation, oppressive and fascist regimes like South Africa or those that have bad reputations as employees, and still get value for your money.

Support businesses that give to charity

Charities are vital links for the community. They spot trouble much faster than governments; they generally support the ordinary person rather than corporations or politicians; and they usually offer extremely good value for money. More and more corporations are giving charitable donations to environment groups, social services, the arts and education. If you support such companies you will be re-investing in charity. Beware of paying twice for a service, however: the Government, not charitable bodies, should pay for essentials.

Give 5 per cent of your income to a deserving cause

In the USA the average amount given to charity is 2.4 per cent of an annual income. It is much less in Britain. Most of us could live on 5 per cent less. Try it for six months (you can get charity donations deducted at source). Get to know the groups and organizations that you want to support.

Don't invest in arms

The great nations of the world spend $1 trillion on defence a year. The folly and waste that goes into servicing a system continually prepared to kill, while millions starve, is inhumane and barbaric. There is only one planet. Nuclear arms, nerve gases, bombs and rockets kill and maim, and they have the power to destroy our ecosystem. We should be putting our spare cash and scientific energy into solving our environmental crises instead of creating new ones. Don't invest in war: boycott companies that manufacture armaments.

Write to the World Bank/IMF

Every second over 0.4 hectare (1 acre) of tropical forest goes up in smoke. Since 1960 we have lost over 40 per cent of the world's tropical forests, the habitat of the world's most beautiful and rarest plant and animal species and the home of approximately 150 million indigenous people whose lives depend on them for survival. Through taxes and government contributions your money goes to the World Bank/IMF: ask the World Bank/IMF in Washington DC to swap the debt that is owed to them by these countries for the protection of the rainforests.

Stocks and shares for the environment

A good broker will be able to advise you how to buy stocks and shares in green companies. Your investment will support them and, with luck, will earn you interest at the same time. Companies such as the Body Shop have seen their share price rise by over 200 per cent in just a few years as more and more bodies have been willing to invest in green businesses.

Organize a credit union

Cooperatively run credit unions can make a real difference to the poor. Loans may attract as little as 12 per cent interest, compared with the normal 24–36 per cent for credit cards and up to 1,000 per cent for a highly profiteering loan shark. Credit unions operate by sharing money according to need, on the principle that profit isn't necessarily their most important goal. The interest pays for the union to operate rather than for profit for companies or individuals.

Tell your bank what you want

Why do banks and building societies continue to send us mailing after mailing about new loans and new insurance plans and invite us to borrow more and more? What a waste of paper! Ask your bank to take your name off their mailing list; ask it to provide cheque books and statements on recycled paper, as there isn't any justification for bleached new paper for these. And what about facilities for disabled people? Banks hardly go out of their way to accommodate even the able-bodied – they must be a nightmare for others. Don't forget: the money you put into them is what they live on. You are the customer, and you are entitled to ask for what you want.

Change policy from the top

Ask financial businesses to take the environment seriously. Banks, building societies and loan companies could all be asked to account for their environmental performance. Ask them to present an environmental report in their annual report to shareholders. Ask them to name one person on their board of directors who would be responsible for the environment.

Ask for environmental audits for loans

Ask your bank or building society to consider environmental audits for new loans, then a list of acceptable criteria could be drawn up and preference given to loans for less damaging or polluting schemes and businesses. Lending institutions are responsible for giving away billions every year, most of it for new homes but a large percentage for home improvements, cars and new businesses. Just think what a difference it would make if you had to answer a question on your loan form about the effect your loan would have on the environment.

Ensure a greener future for your children

Give your children a greener future by investing your savings for them in an environmentally conscious fund. Ask your bank or building society to suggest one: it could be an investment for more than your child alone.

Write to your bank about debt in the Third World

Write to your bank about Third World debt. Is the board of your high-street bank doing anything about Third World debt, and is it prepared to write off the debt in favour of environmentally sustaining projects? Most high-street banks are involved in developing countries, and they are sensitive about what you think of their reputation.

Safeguard your possessions

There are now green insurance funds. They can provide you with insurance cover for your house and car that uses an ethical investment service. They work along the same lines as other ethical investment programmes: your money will not be invested in arms manufacture, tobacco, military dictatorships, South Africa or the support of environmentally destructive programmes. Ask your insurance broker to find out for you.

Bequeath your money to the future

When you write a will or bequest, think about leaving some of your money to environmental groups and organizations. This could make a huge difference especially to smaller organizations, which don't attract the attention of larger groups. Many groups will advise you about how to write a will if you don't know where to start.

Guarantee an assurance that is ethical

Life-assurance funds are common for partners when they buy property jointly: if one partner should die, the life assurance will cover the other partner financially. Ask your life-assurance broker to find you a green fund. This will mean that from the start your money will be invested in sound businesses and environment-conscious trust funds.

Retire in greener pastures

Many jobs include pension funds as a matter of course, and billions are invested in such funds by powerful brokers around the world. At the end of 1989 the total value of UK pension funds was £295 billion. You may argue that your money should be invested in ethical funds for you. The law of fiduciary trust, however, means that your company is required by law to provide its investment members with 'the best available rate of return', which sometimes cuts out some of the ethical funds, especially the newer ones. But where you can influence your company, do so. You can transfer your funds, and pension advice schemes will readily give advice on how to do this.

Choose a responsible way to share your wealth

If you inherit or own some money and you want to share it with others, choose an issue that worries you most. It's worth spending time talking to people and informing yourself thoroughly about the matter before you make your final decision. There are groups of people who meet and share ideas about giving money away responsibly in Britain and the USA. You could help to influence the future by supporting groups and individuals generously.

Order a greening loan

Pressurize your bank or building society into lending you money to use for greener projects – fitting your home with all the latest energy-saving equipment, for example. This investment would be repaid within a few years and would add to the value of the home, so it would be well worth it. If lending agencies were greener, we might see this sort of loan being given in preference to loans for other house improvements, and fewer new power stations would be needed.

Green up your bank

Is your bank investing your money in environmentally sustainable projects? Some banks have been exposed for investing, directly and indirectly, in programmes that destroy rainforests in Brazil; others have invested in dam projects that have destroyed local ecosystems in Asia and South America. Before you open a new account with a bank, ask it to give you an account of its practices. Choose to open an ethical and environmentally sound deposit account that invests only in cooperatives.

Take a green credit card

If you have to use a credit card, why not use it to support one of your favourite groups? Credit cards are becoming increasingly popular with larger organizations as a method of collecting funds. One of the main problems they encounter, however, is a moral one: should they support spending and consumerism? If you are able to live with that dilemma and you need a card, then do at least get a green one.

Get advice

In Britain a growing number of ethical investment services offer advice on specific investments. They should be approved by appropriate professional bodies, so do ask before you take advice from them. They will be able to tell you about the ethical or socially responsible funds available on the market, and they will advise about green pension funds, personal equity plans and investment funds.

Pay bills by standing order

Ask your bank to pay your bills regularly by standing order. Think of all the paper you will save.

Green Work –
Green Leisure

Green Workplaces

Develop an environmental policy

Over 80 per cent of businesses are small ones, employing between twenty and thirty people. It is easy to develop an environmental policy in small workplaces or offices. Start raising general environmental awareness by asking questions, and do not accept 'no' for an answer. Saving the environment can very often save your company money, by using energy efficiency programmes or recycling schemes.

Begin with an Environmental-Impact Assessment

Environmental-Impact Assessments (EIAs) ensure that, when large projects are at the early stages of planning and feasibility studies, possible effects on the environment are taken into account. All businesses should aim to limit environmental degradation from the outset. At present, certain businesses in Europe, including crude-oil refineries, power stations, installations for storing and disposing toxic and dangerous wastes, trading ports and inland waterways, chemical installations and steelworks, are required by an EEC directive to carry out EIAs. All businesses should carry out an Environmental-Impact Assessment at the planning stage. It allows better choices to be made, and it is still early enough to modify the original scheme.

Have a smoke-free office

Millions of people smoke in workplaces across the country. Not only do they inflict a series of health risks on their colleagues but they are also directly responsible for causing pollution. Tobacco production and manufacturing processes include: heavy use of pesticides on the tobacco-plant leaves; the bleaching of cigarette papers; the pollution of rivers and the air. Smokers also pollute their own bodies, running all sorts of health risks which cost your company money in sick pay: a report by the Dow Chemical Company showed that smokers had 80 per cent more sick leave than non-smokers. Smoking is also a fire hazard. Negotiate a smoke-free workplace and help smokers kick the habit that may otherwise eventually kill them.

Ventilate your photocopier

Ozone can be an indoor pollutant, especially if you work in a room without adequate ventilation near photocopiers that are switched on all day. Ozone can be damaging to both the mucous-membranes and the eyes, and it is also thought to cause persistent headaches. Use your photocopier with care, and always ventilate rooms.

Is your building sick?

Artificial lighting, open-plan offices and artificial ventilating systems can create an alarming new illness: Sick Building Syndrome. Sick buildings have been noted in modern office buildings that have artificially created atmospheres. Space-age office machinery has added to the problem, together with chemical fumes, electrostatic interference and electrical risks. It all adds up to a pretty unpleasant atmosphere for workers, who complain of general malaise, lethargy, headaches and the like. This affects productivity and it is therefore in your employer's interest to improve conditions. Check your building. If you think it is sick, take measures to make it better. Contact health and hazard organizations for help.

Don't type so fast!

New technology might save paper, but it can also make you ill as your body attempts to keep up with the speed of the technology itself. Work-related upper-limb disorders or repetitive strain injuries (RSI) affect workers who use electronic keyboards or supermarket bar-code readers. Injuries to the tendons, muscles and joints can result, and this can eventually lead to the loss of use of hands or arms. Operators who are paid piecework rates are most at risk. A typist will average 10,000 keystrokes per hour, but some workplaces offer incentives of extra pay or holidays, and organize competitions, thus pushing typists into producing an excessive 27,000 keystrokes per hour. Computers that can monitor performance are putting extra pressure on workers to go faster and faster. Make sure your chair is angled correctly in front of the VDU, do not agree to excessive speeds for typing and take a break as often as possible.

Get a shield or filter for your VDU

Computer terminals and VDUs have caused problems for workers, as it has been discovered that they emit low-level radiation. They have also been linked to increasing numbers of miscarriages, and other illnesses have been reported, including headaches and skin rashes. I fitted a filter screen on the office computer and the rashes and 'hot' faces were gone within a day. Always take a break after an hour spent working on computers, work for no more than four hours a day in front of a screen and contact trade union and health groups, who have information booklets about the risks.

Do you really need sprays to clean your telephone?

Shared work telephones could possibly spread bacteria or bugs, but cleaning chemicals may be more toxic than your own germs. Aerosol cleaners, even now with 'soft' CFCs or hydrocarbons (another greenhouse gas), are mixed with highly toxic and flammable disinfectants which should not be inhaled in excessive amounts. It is far safer to wipe the telephone with a clean, damp cloth, and it is cheaper too.

Cut the neon lighting

Neon lighting was discovered in 1898. Neon is an odourless gas that can be illuminated in a tube. Added powders alter the state of the gas, producing the full spectrum of coloured lights we now know. Some shops use different types of high-tech laser and computer lighting to sell their wares, but all of them are wasteful of energy and produce tonnes of pollution in the form of carbon dioxide and other greenhouse gases. See if you can do with less neon.

Lighting for health

Our eyes suffer from continuous strain in office situations. Reading from bad photocopies, illegible writing and carbonated papers all put strain on the eyes, but this causes far less strain than the lighting itself. Artificial lighting in offices attempts, without much success, to replace natural light. White fluorescent strip lights can have a constant flicker and can cause headaches, eyestrain and concentration problems. Desk lamps offer some flexibility and create less glare. Using energy-efficient lighting means that you use twice the amount of light for less money. You can have both a good clear light for work and save energy too.

Have an energy-efficient workplace

Saving energy in your workplace will save your company money but can also contribute to reducing global warming by reduced carbon-dioxide emissions. Don't leave office lights on at night. Use compact fluorescent bulbs, which save money and have low wattage. Turn off machines not in use, especially computers and photocopiers. Install efficient heating equipment. Make someone responsible for energy saving in your office.

Ban the vending machine

The hot-drinks vending machine was brought into offices

in the last fifty years, mostly to replace the expensive tea-lady in larger firms and companies. It serves synthetic drinks, powdered milks, coffee and tea, mostly in plastic cups. The few minutes' time a vending machine saves staff are lost on energy costs alone. The average vending machine guzzles electricity – it may be the largest single user of energy in the workplace. Using mugs and low-energy water-urns might be a better option and give you tastier drinks.

Static-free floors

Increasing numbers of complaints have been recorded in workplaces about a strange new 'bug' found in artificial carpets. Synthetic backings (foam underlays may contain CFCs) and plastic coatings encourage carpets to attract static. This in turn has been 'jumping' up and 'attacking' workers on the legs. The build-up of static electricity is further encouraged by the use of VDUs and other machinery. A natural carpet with hessian backing will reduce the static immediately. Using little or no synthetic chemicals in the coatings and as cleaners also helps.

Use long-life equipment

It is obvious that office equipment that is used by many people needs to be hardwearing to be economic, but the better the equipment you buy, the better for the environment. Use materials like metal filing cabinets instead of paper or card ones. Buy from secondhand shops, which is also a form of recycling – and cheaper, too!

Catch the cheap desk out

Cheap veneer desks can harbour numerous environmental

hazards. They have chipboard interiors and, although chipboard is rarely made from rainforest wood, it is usually bonded with formaldehyde glues that can cause problems if they seep out. The veneers are likely to be from rainforest-wood sources, however, unless they are plastic laminates, which attract dust and dirt. Solid wood desks from sustainable sources are the best to use. You can even have them waxed and varnished with organic materials, for easier care.

Don't demand a rainforest-wood desk

Over 90 per cent of the tropical hardwoods used in Britain come from the rainforests. This means that your new desk, and the chair you sit in, may well be from a rainforest source. Check out where the wood used in your office furniture comes from. Avoid hardwoods, especially if you can't discover the country of origin. Use the Friends of the Earth *Good Wood Guide* to help you.

CFC-free office furniture

It is not just aerosols that contain CFCs – chemicals that destroy the ozone layer. The foam used for most office chairs contains these chemicals. Check on this with your supplier. The chairs should also conform to strict fire-safety measures, as the burning foam can give off toxic fumes.

Audit your suppliers

You get what you ask for! Why not start auditing your suppliers? Do they stock recycled paper? Water-based pens? Energy-efficient lighting? The equipment and furniture that you buy to keep your workplace going needs to be environmentally sound. Ask your suppliers to offer you the best possible alternatives to environmentally damaging products.

Don't use envelopes with plastic windows

Envelopes with plastic windows are the most environmentally unfriendly envelopes available. They are not recyclable and are likely to be made of virgin paper. Ordinary brown envelopes are mostly made from recycled pulp. If you have started to recycle paper in your office, you will find that window envelopes are not acceptable. Encourage your stationery-buyer and your post department not to use them – they are more expensive anyway.

Disposable writing

Every day rubbish bins in the USA contain 4,383,562 disposable pens. Around the world, the throw-away ballpoint pen has become a familiar part of our lives. Made of plastic, non-biodegradable and rarely used right until the ink is finished, they are an environmental hazard that also wastes precious fossil fuels. Try using a refillable pen, cut down on disposables, or, if you must use them, don't throw them away until they are completely finished.

Correct your correcting fluid

Have you ever wondered what is in that lovely white correcting fluid you use for your typing errors? The main chemical is 11-trichloroethane, also known as methyl chloroform, a toxic and irritant chemical that depletes the ozone layer and stays around for a long time in the environment. It is particularly dangerous when burnt, as it forms phosgene gas. Look for water-based whiteners that say specifically that they have removed tri-chloroethane. If you can't find a good alternative, cut down your use of them.

★

Save paper

It is estimated that businesses in the USA use over 1.6 trillion sheets of paper each year; around 13 per cent of these are unnecessary photocopies. A waste of several million trees. Add the energy bill to that and you will see that the photo-copy machine seems to have created a wasteful problem. Cut down on the amount of photocopies you make, re-use paper written on only one side for notes and always keep a bin next to the copier in which to place spoiled sheets for recycling.

Use clear glues

Adhesives, sticky tapes and other glues are big business. One giant company recently sold its worldwide adhesives opera-tion for £100 million, for just one brand. Glues are a very necessary part of the office, but some are more toxic than others. Glue production itself can lead to environmental prob-lems, as the volatile chemicals can escape into waterways and river systems. Glues can contain phenol, vinyl chloride, formal-dehyde and epoxy resins, naphthalene and other harmful chemicals. They are often addictive and volatile. Avoid them as much as possible. Stick to white glues and simple-formula woodworking glues whenever possible.

Don't use coloured paperclips

Paperclips are a small but necessary item in the office. They can be recycled and re-used many times, which makes them valuable and cost-effective, but say no to the coloured paper-clips that are dipped in bright plastics. They can contain cadmium, a toxic heavy metal.

Use water-based and felt-tip pens

Graphic artists are among those who will use coloured pens

most these days, but all offices and workplaces are using increasingly sophisticated means of communication: wipe-clear boards, notices, documents that need sections highlighted need good quality colouring pens. Permanent-ink markers contain solvents and chemicals like phenol-toluene and xylene. They are moderately toxic if swallowed and must be used with care in well-ventilated rooms. Prolonged exposure to these chemicals can cause dizziness, and toluene may have effects on the central nervous system that could be dangerous. Opt for water-based markers whenever possible.

Run down the battery use

When manufacturing batteries, up to fifty times more energy than the batteries actually produce is used. Offices and work-places around the world regularly use batteries to operate calculators, clocks and machines. Use mains-operated equipment, solar-powered calculators and hand-operated machinery whenever possible. If you must use batteries, try 'green' rechargeable ones, which last up to 500 times longer.

Check your continuous stationery

Computers were hailed as the new technology that would rid us of unwanted paper forever. Waste was going to be a thing of the past. Unfortunately, it never really worked like that. Computer stationery ended up making us waste even more than we used to. Machines using sprockets for continuous stationery seem to be the worst, as there is often no way to stop them when in mid-flow. Collect your unwanted computer stationery in a bin near the computer; it is the most highly valued for recycling. Use single-sheet feeders whenever you can, and cut down on the numbers of sheets that are printed out whenever possible. Recycled computer stationery is available.

Use recycled soft-paper products

Toilet paper and paper towels should not be made from paper pulp from new trees, nor should the paper be bleached. Recycled paper products save your company money and protect the environment at the same time. See if you can cut down on the numbers of paper towels that are used, and switch to recycled paper products wherever possible.

Get rid of the plastic mailout

Magazines and newspapers in plastic bags are being mailed to subscribers all over the world. Literally millions of these bags are used each day. If your workplace sends mailouts with plastic wrappers ask your employer to return to recycled paper wrapping. These flimsy plastic bags are not biodegradable and are estimated to last for 400 years in landfill sites. Recycled paper, on the other hand, can be recycled again and represents a better use of resources. The publishers of American magazines like the *New Yorker* and *Mother Jones* have already bowed to public pressure and concern about the environment and have reverted to paper once more. If you receive magazines in plastic mailouts, write to the publisher.

Avoid styrofoam coffee cups

Styrofoam cups, together with styrofoam plates and containers from the canteen, should be avoided. They are made with CFCs, which destroy the ozone layer, and they cannot be recycled. Bring in your own mug and ask the canteen to switch to recyclable paper plates.

*

Reduce noise at work

Noise can be a pollution problem. It can damage the ears and add to stress at work. Machines clicking, vibrating and humming, telephones ringing, typewriters and computers clattering and bleeping all make a noisy environment for the average office worker. Add that to a machine in the background and you could have a real problem. Excessive noise affects your senses; it contributes to headaches, loss of sleep, fatigue and stress. Hearing damage begins at about 75 decibels of noise if continuous, and yet most factories regularly operate at above 90 decibels. Even open-plan offices can reach 80 decibels. Use engineering controls to reduce the noise of machinery, fit acoustic controls like thick carpeting, heavy fabrics and plants which 'absorb' noise. Consider sound-proofing to reduce the exposure of workers to noise pollution.

Beware dangerous chemicals

More than 1 million industrial chemicals are used in British workplaces every day. At least 2,400 of those are suspected of causing cancer, and many more have unknown properties and effects. Office workers are exposed to powders, dust, gases and liquids from machinery and equipment. Factory workers are exposed to even more chemicals in large industrial settings and workers are often ill-informed about their effects. Hazards are likely to increase as more machinery is used. It is your employer's legal responsibility to provide a safe working environment and healthy working conditions for you. Always use the minimum quantity of each chemical, ask about their specific properties, ensure that you have good ventilation and keep a careful eye on the health effects of any chemicals you may be exposed to. Cutting down the number of chemicals used in your workplace cuts down the production of these

chemicals, and therefore the amount of damage they do to the environment, as well as to you.

Don't test fire-extinguishers with halons

Halons are used in certain types of fire-extinguishers, particularly those for use on computers and electrical equipment, because they can smother a fire with a foam without destroying the computer. Although Halon 1211, the chemical usually used in the fire-extinguisher, is non-toxic to humans, it is also a serious ozone depleter. Dr Joe Farman from the British Antarctic Survey believes halons now cause some 14–30 per cent of the ozone depletion over the Antarctic. And 95 per cent of the emissions actually come from testing the extinguishers to identify leaks from accidental releases and from losses from old equipment. This is one place where we can cut emissions radically and immediately. Check that the extinguisher you use is halon-free. Air-pressure testing for leaks is an alternative to releasing these dangerous chemicals.

Ban aerosols

Aerosols are used in cleaning, graphic design, paint-spraying and a host of other office and factory uses. In every case there is a friendlier alternative to this wasteful packaging. Hand pump sprays for paints and glues offer more control; cleaning materials do not need aerosol sprays. Phase out your use of aerosols in the office and you will probably end up saving money. Remember, those aerosols marked ozone-friendly have removed CFCs, but have added other atmospheric pollutants.

Provide disposal facilities for sanitary towels

The 1936 Public Health Act forbids the disposal of any article that might block the flow of the sewage system. Women's toilets must have facilities to dispose of sanitary towels if they are used by more than ten employees or members of the public. There are sound environmental reasons for not flushing sanitary towels down the toilet: after they are passed through the sewage system they end up in our seas and on the beaches. However, more than half of British workplaces have less than 10 employees and are therefore not covered by the Act. Disposal facilities ought to be provided in your workplace as a matter of course.

Recycle your rubbish

Rubbish collected in the workplace can often be more valuable than you think. Discarded computer paper is the most highly prized of all recycled waste, and it fetches a high price. Cans, bottles, even food wastes can be recycled or made into compost for the office garden plot.

Support your cleaner

Cleaners face many hidden hazards in the workplace. Handling detergents and cleaning fluids can lead to skin problems. Solvents used for floor-stripping, window-cleaning and removing graffiti can cause skin irritation, drowsiness or even unconsciousness. Airborne dust causes eye, throat and nose problems. Toxic gases can be formed when bleaches and disinfectants are mixed together. These can cause lung damage. Allergies to cleaning fluids, accidents caused by wet floors, back and knee injuries and the general risk of disease from clearing up our waste often make the cleaners' jobs the worst in any workplace. A large proportion of cleaners are migrant workers, mostly women, who are given little or no training and have few rights and liberties in their workplace. Support should include training, getting rid of toxic cleansers and using safer, environmentally benign alternatives.

Say no to a company car

Unless your job involves deliveries, do not accept a company car as part of your pay package. It costs the taxpayer millions every year in lost income when cars are processed as belonging to the company. The pollution created by these cars amounts to millions of tonnes of carbon dioxide, the most widespread greenhouse gas. If employees in your company need individual transport, make sure it's at least lead-free and buy a new model that has a catalytic converter.

Share your car

If you cannot take the bus or train to work, then do not travel alone in your car. Start a car pool. This way you will be sharing the costs, as well as cutting down on both the pollution emitted and the numbers of cars on the roads by up to 75 per cent.

Provide company bikes!

Why not offer a company bike instead of a company car, which guzzles fuel and pollutes the air? Bikes are much cheaper to buy: even an extremely good bike costs under £400. They have virtually no maintenance costs compared to cars, they create no pollution and they help to keep us fit.

Be kinder to your environment

Workplaces can do a lot for the environment. You can support groups locally, giving donations or goods in kind. You can set aside an area in your grounds to go green, planting trees and encouraging flowers. Have real plants in the office, not plastic ones, and encourage people to look after them. Creating a green environment in your workplace will have positive effects on staff morale and create a genuinely better working atmosphere.

Build a kestrel box

Some birds prefer the warmth of a city. Office blocks and factories can create an artificial home for the kestrel, often to the delight of workers. This magnificent bird, with a wing span of up to 80 cm, is a familiar sight at the sides of roads, where it looks for voles and insects at a height of up to 12 kilometres. In cities kestrels like to nest on top of tall office buildings and you can help them by building a home for them. Around urban areas try looking upwards more often: you may be surprised to spot this reddish-brown falcon.

Tell someone else

Despite the current 'greening' of companies, some workplaces will not give up some of their profits to clean up their act or protect their employees without a fight. Though the Health and Safety at Work legislation provides some protection, a worker who complains may risk being passed over for promotion or even sacked. When the environment or the health of the public or other workers is at risk, profits must come second and someone has to speak up. Get help from outside sources like a lawyer, the Citizens' Advice Bureau or a trade union, and prepare your case. Perhaps you should even consider sending the information to a newspaper to expose extreme practices.

Sport and Leisure

Decide where to eat

Every day 300 million people eat out in restaurants in Europe and America. Where they choose is as important as what they eat. Some 130 million of them opt for fast-food outlets, munching through hamburgers and 'junk food' at amazing rates. Using millions of tonnes of waste paper and plastic, fast-food outlets are spreading around the world, changing the normally healthy diets of the young into food fads. The London Food Commission reckons that every hamburger we eat may contain offal – the internal organs of animals, like the pancreas, stomach, lungs and testicles – and 100 per cent beefburgers can legally contain 30 per cent fat. Fast food is high in sugar, salt and fat, and low in protein and vitamins. Choose well to enjoy your entertainment, do not waste packaging and you could feel better for it, too.

Throw an organic dinner-party

Have everything, from wine to dessert, organic and sugar-free.

Watch human circuses, not animals

We can abuse animals by degrading them to perform for our amusement. In circuses we watch as chimpanzees dressed up in human clothes have tea-parties and jump through rings of fire on roller skates, and tigers, elephants and lions run through hoops, and have whips cracked at them to prove our power over them. These tricks are not always 'amusing' to the animals concerned and stories of inhumane practices and cruelty are not uncommon. We can derive pleasure from watching humans in new-style circuses, such as the world-famous Circus-Oz group from Australia, with their fantastic acrobatics. There is little justification for having animals prance around for our pleasure.

Leave motorboats for the bath

One of the most annoying forms of noise pollution is a high speed toy motorboat in a public pond. Unfortunately this does not just annoy those people who can hear it up to a mile away, but it also upsets and stresses birds and wildlife. This sort of executive toy ends up being a public and environmental nuisance.

Do not collect butterflies

Butterflies are a good indicator of the state of our environment. When they can be found in abundance they show the local ecology is generally in good form. But species have been declining around the world in recent years. Of the 2,300 species of butterflies and moths to be found in Britain, the average person will probably only ever see about 5 per cent. At least 122 species are listed in the Red Data Book as seriously threatened by pesticides, a loss of habitat or climatic changes. Collectors, however, are responsible for acquiring and mounting large numbers of butterflies; it is illegal to collect those that are endangered.

Take photographs

Become an expert in your local community and on holiday. Take photographs of everything. Photos are modern-day records of how we live, and they will perhaps become poignant reminders of wildlife scenes of today. In the USA the National Audubon Society produces a diary with beautiful pictures of wildlife scenes supplied by the public.

Write it down

Much of the poetry and writing we take for granted today has been inspired by nature and by beautiful natural surroundings. D. H. Lawrence and Thomas Hardy, Dervla Murphy and J. D. Salinger have shown us a countryside and world to be admired and loved. Hilda Murrell, the anti-nuclear campaigner, kept an inspiring countryside diary, published after her death. Write about your own area in letters, poems, journals and diaries and send your contributions to local newspapers and community and theatre groups.

Knit it

Knitting can be more than a hobby. Dramatic designs and warming woollies can cheer up just about anyone. Knitting saves money and can also be soothing – and fun! Use good quality pure wools, avoiding those mixes made with petrochemical derivatives. Get yourself some patterns and needles and you're away!

Check the water for watersports

Blue-green algae are causing problems for those who take part in water sports. In 1989 marinas, swimming areas and watersport and sailing centres were closed for weeks as a thick blue-green algae spread over still-water areas in Britain, Canada and some European countries. Local people were taken into hospital with serious illnesses as a result of swallowing the water, and at least twenty-four dogs died in the Anglia region alone. The poisoning is thought to be connected to high phosphate and nitrate levels from sewage and farming in the water, but scientists have yet to pinpoint an exact cause. Individuals are advised not to swim or take part in water-sports in areas affected by these algae.

Use lead-free fishing weights

Every year in the USA some 5,479 waterfowl are poisoned by lead, mostly from fishing weights used by enthusiastic anglers. These are now restricted in Britain because of the serious loss of swans they have caused. Angling is still the leading sport in the UK, and in the last few years much concern has been raised about the vast numbers of anglers discarding lead weights into waterways around the country. Lead can be a killer. It is possible to use tungsten polymer or tin rubber polymer alternatives. If you still use lead – stop.

Watch your nets

Serious anglers who use special nets or lobster creels for catching fish could be responsible for killing over 100 otters every year in Britain. The otters look in the nets for food and an unattended basket becomes a death trap.

Check your boats

If you are lucky enough to own a boat or yacht, then you will have to be especially careful about using anti-fouling agents like parachlorometacresol, which is highly toxic and has been found to create long-term environmental damage and pollution. Be especially vigilant with chemicals that you do not know, and use only the minimum amount necessary. Tributylin compounds were banned for small boats in 1987 in Britain but are still permitted on larger ships. They have been found to be persistent pollutants, causing damage to oyster beds and dog-whelk populations.

Anglers – protect the water first

Anglers, who are often the first to notice a decline in the diversity of aquatic life, an indication that the water is poisoned, can get involved and campaign for a cleaner water. Pollution from industry kills aquatic life.

Do you need to watch the dolphins?

Popular display cetaceans are the killer whale, the rough-toothed dolphin, the pilot whale and the bottlenose dolphins. There is widespread concern over the physical and mental stress this can cause, and the high mortality rate of captive cetaceans. Some 4,580 small cetaceans have been caught so far for display and research. They may look beautiful in a pool, but they are far happier at home in the ocean. Do not encourage the spectacle of watching these beautiful creatures perform tricks for our cheap amusement.

A-hunting we won't go

Mink hunting could be endangering the otter even further. It is not illegal to hunt an otter, but it is to kill it. Because of this the mink has become a ready substitute for hunters. They are followed by packs of hounds along river banks causing disturbances and panic not just among the mink, but among all other wildlife in the vicinity. This 'sport' is carried out between the end of one fox-hunting season and the start of another. There is no scientific or historical reason for hunting mink or otters.

Harehunting and coursing is not necessary

The hare population in Britain is in a serious state of decline, the major factors being habitat destruction and intentional slaughter. Deliberate killing of hares is a needless and bloody sport. Hunting enthusiasts train a pack of dogs to run the hare to exhaustion for about an hour and a half. This 'sport' is organized, well funded and barbaric. There is no justification for it.

Foxes are not pests

It is widely believed that foxes are a threat to agriculture, and yet the feeding habits of foxes are actually a benefit to the farmer. Foxes eat rabbits, rats, voles, earthworms, insects, beetles, fallen fruit and the carcasses of wild and domestic animals and birds. They will take advantage of badly housed poultry, but according to the Ministry of Agriculture predation on lambs by foxes is 'insignificant' at 5 per cent: 10–24 per cent of lambs die from hypothermia, malnutrition or diseases. Rogue foxes can be shot or caught in human traps by farmers, but foxhunting has the same purpose as dog-baiting and bear-baiting and should be considered barbaric. The violent and bloody death of foxes for sport should not be supported.

Look after golf courses

Golf courses are great places for wildlife, provided pesticides aren't sprayed over them. The land set aside for this sport makes a significant potential wildlife reservoir. Unimproved 'rough' lands are the most prolific in wild creatures and offer a haven for rare species like the natterjack toad and great crested newt. Badgers and foxes like to breed in this terrain and the number of birds frequenting these areas increases every year. Protect the wildlife of the golf course: don't spray pesticides and chemicals. If you are a member of a club, then make sure committees and stewards know of the importance of their land.

Sunbeds are a hazard

The American Medical Association produced warnings in 1985 against the continued use of sunbeds. In their report they concluded that 'there is no known medical benefit obtained from cosmetic tanning. Exposure to high intensity UVA radiation in the tanning booths currently in vogue is a health hazard'. Standards for sunbed users are scarce, especially for those who use them at home. Most specialists advise people who care about their skin to avoid using sunbeds. A *Which?* report concluded that at least one in five home sunbed-users does not use the protective goggles that are essential to protect you against eye damage.

On the Road

Do without the car

During 1987 there were more than 400 million cars in the world, mostly in North America and Europe. They use one-third of the world's petrol and produce one-half of all the world's air pollution. Cars cost £8 billion each year through traffic congestion, £3 billion each year through accidents and they cause 5,500 serious accidents each year in Britain alone. The car is the most dangerous, uneconomic and environmentally polluting form of transport that has ever been invented. Isn't it time you looked at the alternatives? The suggestions below should be looked at if you feel you really *need* the car, but its use cannot be endorsed.

Forget the parking – leave your car at home

Parking places near shopping centres and offices are becoming increasingly expensive. You can pay £20 a day to park in London or over £5,000 per year. A parking space in a New York City condominium garage will set you back $29,000. In Toronto, Canada, the city authorities have encouraged high parking prices to dissuade people from using their cars in the city because of excess pollution, traffic jams and accidents. Next time you go to town, leave your car behind and the land space now used for parking lots can be converted to more ecologically sound uses.

Take the bus!

A bus can carry nearly a hundred passengers for less fuel than a single car. Clearly, one bus takes up less room than the hundred cars needed to carry the same passengers if they were driving on their own. If only 5 per cent of our car journeys were made by bus, we could use 250,000 fewer tonnes of dangerous emissions like carbon monoxide, sulphur dioxide, nitrous oxide and lead every year. Buses are cheaper than cars, and the more people use them, campaign for them and insist on them, the more buses there will be. So, next time, take the bus.

Use your feet

Walking is a very important part of our lives. About 74 per cent of all recorded journeys are of 8 kilometres (4 miles) or less, and most of those are on foot. During the recent tube strike in London, many people started to walk to work and discovered that they actually enjoyed it, but the state of the roads is a frequent hazard. A walker is more likely to be killed on the road by a passing car than a car passenger is, and yet we give little opportunity for safety on the roads for pedestrians. Kerb and pavement maintenance, pavement parking, dog excrement and lack of safe crossing places are just some of the problems for the average pedestrian.

Hire a car

There may well be times when you just can't do the things you want to without a car. Why not find a good car-hire firm and hire a car as and when you need it? Make sure the car runs on lead-free petrol and has a catalytic converter. It works out cheaper in the long run, as you don't have to pay for road tax, insurance, garage fees, etc. Be sure to look after the car, though: a car abused by many drivers lasts only a short time.

Cycle for safety, cycle for the planet

Cycling is by far the most energy-efficient form of transport ever invented. Bicycles are cheaper to manufacture than cars, easier to park, safer for pedestrians, produce no pollution and are easy to maintain. Go by bike – there just isn't a better way to travel.

Cycle round your town

A cycling demonstration is a great way of gaining support

from other cyclists and swelling the number of cyclists in your area. Get together a group of cyclists to cycle round your town. Survey potential cycle lanes and lobby your local authority. What about asking other cyclists to sign a petition for better facilities?

Let the train take the strain

The number of people using rail travel in the UK is increasing even though public subsidy is decreasing. The current government policy is to reduce the subsidy to zero in the next few years. Across the rest of Europe we see an altogether different picture. Turin in Italy comes top with a subsidy of 87 per cent and Rome and Rotterdam second with 81 per cent. For long-distance travelling, the train is the most efficient and cleanest form of travel. And it is often the pleasantest: you can walk around while the train is moving, travel easily and safely with children, eat and even sleep on the train. Campaign for a re-instatement of the train subsidy, get polluting cars off the motorways and get people back in the railway carriages!

Get a ticket

A railcard, travelcard or season ticket will encourage you to use public transport and keep your costs down. It makes life easier for conductors and ticket collectors, and this in turn speeds up human traffic on platforms and on the bus. The income from regular season-ticket holders allows the transport system to plan ahead, which means a better service. Last but not least, you waste less paper by having only one ticket per month or year, not two or three a day.

Share a car

You may not own a car, but you could still have access to

one if you need it. How about sharing one car with several friends who live nearby? Or linking up with community centres or organizations to 'loan' cars when you really need them?

Avoid driving in bad weather

Avoid driving in bad weather, not just because of the added risk of accidents, but because there is around a 3 per cent fuel loss for each 6 °C (10 °F) drop in temperature. Driving in the rain and snow reduces petrol economy by about 10 per cent, and the wind reduces mileage. Try to make your journey at another time and, if this is impossible, think about taking public transport as an alternative.

Avoid using a car in cities

Driving your car in a city uses at least twice as much fuel as driving a similar distance on the motorway. The average speed is often about 16 kilometres (10 miles) per hour in cities like London – which is slower than the horse and cart of a hundred years ago! With buses, taxis, bicycles, tubes and walking as alternatives, your car should be bottom of the list in a city.

Take the junk out of your car

Before you set off on a long drive, check your car. You may feel that it is vitally important to carry around your tools and a spare battery, but the lighter your car, the less fuel it will burn and the less pollution it will create. Every 45 kilograms (100 lb) of extra weight decreases petrol efficiency by 1 per cent.

Buy a 'greener' car

If you can't live without a car then you should shop around

and buy a car that does as little damage to the environment as possible. Buy one that is able to run on lead-free petrol and has a three-way catalytic converter. Make sure it is fuel-efficient and do not buy a car that is larger than you need. This could be one of the biggest choices you make for the environment, so do it well and with all the necessary information. Get in touch with environment groups that campaign on car use and collect your information carefully.

Consider a secondhand car

A secondhand car may initially be cheaper to buy, but it could cost you much more to run. The older an engine becomes, the less efficient it is and the more fuel and oil guzzling it becomes. The life-span of cars has decreased very quickly. Cars are made with built-in-obsolescence in mind, so that you must buy a new one more often. Secondhand cars tend to need more work and more attention than new ones.

Install a catalytic converter

If you have to have a car, then you should consider buying a catalytic converter, which will cut the emissions of carbon monoxide and nitrogen oxides from each car by 75 per cent. The gases emitted by cars cause serious damage, such as acid rain and the greenhouse effect, which contributes to the warming of our planet. It is vital that we consider the use of catalytic converters. A British company, Johnson Matthey, is one of the leading manufacturers of catalytic converters world-wide, yet produces most of these for overseas markets.

Avoid short trips in cars

The easiest way to waste petrol is to set out on a cold day for a short trip in your car. You can squander all the precious fuel you have saved by looking after the vehicle and being safety conscious. Cold weather means that you will have a longer warm-up time for the car, wasting fuel further. Walk or cycle for short journeys.

Check your brakes

The brakes on your car are a vital component and you should check them regularly. A loss of brake fluid is the commonest type of brake failure, and is caused by leaks in the hydraulic system. Check the fluid level regularly and you will save fuel and energy – as well as your life.

Look after your car

British law states that a car must comply with the certain requirements for road-worthiness by passing a Ministry of Transport (MOT) test. Most cars must be tested annually, but to save energy and cut down on pollution your car should be regularly tested and maintained anyway. A car tuning could give you a 5 per cent fuel-usage improvement, and checking on brakes, reflectors, tyres, seat-belts, exhaust, indicators, shock-absorbers and lights all ensure that your car is not a safety hazard.

Plan your trip

Plan your trip carefully in order to use the minimum amount of fuel necessary. Travelling during non-peak hours, having to stop at the least number of traffic lights helps save on fuel. Avoid crowded cities as much as you can. Call your auto club and get help with planning the trip.

Recycle CFCs in cars

An air-conditioner in a car causes an average release into the atmosphere of 1.1 kilograms (2.5 lb) of CFCs per car each year, according to the US-based Greenhouse Crisis Foundation. Recharging your air-conditioner causes another 0.4 kilogram (1 lb) to be released. This is one of the main sources of chlorofluorocarbon emissions in the United States and, as more and more cars are fitted with air-conditioners across Europe, the problem will escalate. Machines are available that can recycle and save the CFCs during the service and repair of your air-conditioner. Insist that this is done.

Use the best quality oil

Using oil in your car is vital for a long-lasting, efficient engine. The better the quality, the more fuel-efficient your car will be, as this reduces engine friction. You should change the oil as often as is recommended by the manufacturer. Keep a record of each change, for easy reference.

Use unleaded petrol

In Britain we currently put out over 2,500 tonnes of lead through our car exhausts every year, though levels are falling. This contributes to serious illnesses, including brain damage in young children. As a bonus, lead-free petrol is cheaper, and over 45 per cent of British cars are now suitable for lead-free petrol. Start using unleaded petrol immediately if you have not already done so, and if your car will run on it. Many companies provide free or extremely cheap conversions.

Stick to 88 kilometres per hour (55 m.p.h.)

Driving at a steady 88 kilometres (55 miles) per hour on the motorway or road is safer and can reduce the amount of fuel you use. Driving at 112 k.p.h. (70 m.p.h.) will be as much as 25 per cent less efficient in fuel consumption, and thus cause a lot more pollution. Speed, of course, also means that you will be more likely to have an accident.

Check your tyres

Check your car tyres at least once every two weeks and before any long journey. Worn or damaged tyres are both illegal and dangerous. Inspect the treads and walls for flaws and sharp objects. Bulges in the sidewalls are particularly unsafe. When correctly inflated, car tyres can save up to 10 per cent on performance efficiency.

Use radial tyres

Radial tyres can improve your fuel efficiency by as much as 4 per cent when compared to cross-ply tyres.

Use tinted glass in your car windows

According to the government in the USA, new studies show

that light-coloured cars with tinted glass need less air-conditioning than other cars. Avoid buying a car with air-conditioning if you can; they all use CFCs, which damage the ozone layer. An air-conditioner uses more fuel per mile as well, costing more money and causing more pollution and it is not really necessary in Britain. Why not ask about solar-powered air-conditioning, now widely available in the USA?

Learn to drive better

A driving instructor I knew once said: 'If only people would come to me and ask me to teach them how to drive safely for the rest of their lives. Instead, they ask me to get them through their driving test.' Our attitude to driving is something that does not only save lives. Slowing down well in advance of traffic, accelerating gradually and driving at a reasonable speed saves petrol and creates less pollution too.

Avoid the 'extras' when you buy a car

These days the huge market for cars means that we are given an ever-increasing number of 'extras' to entice us into buying a particular model: electronic windows, gadgets and devices for every conceivable whim, from lighting a cigarette to turning over your cassettes. All of these, plus others such as power steering, power brakes and air-conditioning add weight to the vehicle and increase the amount of engine power needed to run it.

Warm up without air-conditioning

The biggest users of air-conditioning are cars, in which CFC-12 is used – which is an ozone depleter. The CFCs can be released when the system leaks or in the fitting of the air-conditioning unit, and the mixtures of CFC-12 and DME azeotrope, which is being presented as a substitute for CFCs, still cause problems, as they are greenhouse gases. Do not buy a new car with air-conditioning. This may be very hard to do in extremely hot countries, but certainly not in Britain!

Recycle your car tyres

Recycling schemes for car tyres save energy and resources but are under-utilized. When you recycle 1 kilogram (2.2 lb) of rubber from a tyre you can save up to 71 per cent of the energy it takes to produce rubber from plantations. In the USA, where some 657,534 million tyres are produced every day, only 197,260 are recycled per annum. Companies are starting to introduce recycling schemes, and most tyres now contain about 10 per cent recycled rubber. Ask when you next get your tyres changed.

Keep off the pavement

Some car drivers park on the pavement because it stops their cars from being hit, especially on narrow roads, and sometimes because of sheer laziness. But it is a hazard, causing millions of pounds-worth of damage to kerbs and walkways not originally built for tonnes of metal. It also causes havoc for pedestrians, especially the blind and disabled, and those with children in push-chairs. Park sensibly, and walk the extra few minutes if necessary.

Don't support new road-building schemes

In California, the Department of Transport admitted, after spending \$61 billion on new roads, that no further road-building would ensure free movement for drivers. Every day in Britain enough new cars are bought to make a ten-mile traffic jam, and from them a further 250,000 tonnes of carbon dioxide, the principal greenhouse gas, is churned out. Successive governments have thought they could solve the crisis by building more roads; they still have not learned better. Study after study has proved that all new road-building schemes help for a short time only, but then they attract more cars, vans and heavy lorries, and simply aggravate congestion and create even more pollution. Do not support new road schemes, do not drive unless absolutely necessary, especially in cities, and you will stop the madness of the new roads.

Allow 'traffic calming'

Five and a half thousand people are seriously injured or killed in Britain on roads in built-up areas each year. Cars have been regarded as more important than pedestrians for a long time, making roads and cars the main feature of our communities. Pedestrians lose out. Pollution, noise and lack of safety are just some of the problems. Many roads in residential areas could be closed off to cars. 'Traffic-calming' schemes include road humps, creating pedestrian areas, building wider roads to allow one-way traffic only and using bricks and cobblestones to create a different road surface (which makes cars slow down). All these measures can be carried out by local councils and officials, but they must be agreed by residents. You could put these ideas forward and argue for a better environment for your area.

Don't drop litter from your car

There's nothing worse for a cyclist or pedestrian (or even another car driver) to see than a driver winding down a window and throwing out cigarette butts or sweet wrappers. It's not simply a bad habit. It's an environmental hazard. Don't do it.

Don't salt the drive

In freezing weather ice and snow can be dangerous, but using salt to clear your drive and country or city roads can have environmental effects. Nearby water becomes salinated and can harm wildlife. It also damages your car. In very cold countries salt is sometimes necessary, but in Britain grit is usually more than adequate.

Paper aeroplanes

We use staggering amounts of paper in aeroplanes – as napkins, as head rests, as wrappers for food and utensils. All of it is, of course, bleached white and made from trees. Next time you fly, try saving as much paper as you can – don't take it in the first place. I find that if I take the paper and try to hand it back unused it is always just thrown away. Every minute of every day there are 1 million people in the air. This means that billions of tonnes of paper are being used and thrown away – or not used and thrown away – and literally millions of trees are unnecessarily destroyed.

Use coins in phone boxes

Why use disposable plastic to make your telephone call when reusable coins will often do? In the USA you can often use your credit card, which means that you save by using only one piece of disposable plastic instead of the millions that are used in Britain by our throw-away phonecards. Credit cards can now be used on some new phone systems in Britain, so watch out for them, but use coins whenever you can. Ask British Telecom to extend the credit-card phone systems.

On Holiday

Don't book a package holiday

In the usual course of events, package-tour operators have little or no sensitivity for local environments or communities so long as they are clean and holiday-makers enjoy themselves. In 1989 12.5 million Britons went off to exotic-sounding countries like Greece, Turkey or the Seychelles. Unfortunately, the whole infrastructure that must be set up to allow mass tourism takes its toll on the local people and environment. If there is a recession in Britain, the tour operators want a lower price for the best hotels, which means local people lose out financially. The local communities are then left to deal with the rubbish and waste left behind, while the often badly needed foreign exchange goes to the British tour operators. Do yourself and the country you want to visit a favour, and do not book a package holiday.

Invest in development holidays

Some travel agents act as charities and plough back all of their profits into supporting good, sustainable development projects. One such agency is North–South Travel, which promotes holidays between people in the north (Europe, North America, etc.) and people in the south (India, South Asia, etc.). By booking your holiday through them you could be supporting worthwhile projects in the country you visit as well.

Support holiday firms that care about the environment

There is a growing number of holiday companies that plough back profits and resources into the environment. Some operate in the country where the holiday is to take place, for example they support wildlife sanctuaries and conservation groups. Some help fund key research projects that study the effects of man on the environment. You can support these companies by booking your holiday through them, and asking your regular agent to consider similar kinds of support.

Choose an unusual holiday for adventure

Did you know that there are 92,000 North Americans on a waiting list to go to the moon? Most of us expect some interest and enjoyment from our precious holidays but the thought of being shot into space is definitely not for me. Choosing holidays that will have little impact on the environment (travelling to the moon fails miserably on this score), means proper planning and organization beforehand. Trekking and camping trips are great as long as you are not planning to tramp through an ancient woodland growing orchids. Holidays planned with sensitivity take into account the environment rather than intrude on it. Adventure holidays are best when you leave the area intact for others to enjoy.

Take an activity break

Rock-climbing, pony trekking, hill-walking, sailing, canoeing and mountaineering – all are invigorating experiences for those who prefer an activity holiday. There are hundreds of choices and most seek to instil a healthy respect for the environment as an important part of the break – and there's always space for beginners!

Go on a pick-your-own farm holiday

There are still a number of farms with 'pick-your-own' facilities, and they often have a wide variety of fruit and vegetables. You can mix the pleasure of a holiday with the pleasure of choosing your own fresh food. Of course, this is only good as a holiday when the particular crop you are interested in is in season. Perhaps everyone should have a two-week holiday at harvest time, to get the best fruits and vegetables in season in order to pick, bottle and preserve ready for the coming winter months.

Don't choose hunting holidays

Hunting holidays provide a most barbaric form of pleasure, especially when capturing or killing endangered species is the most important activity. It is estimated that in the USA 250 million wild animals are killed by people on hunting holidays every year. One of the most prized trophies for hunting expeditions in South America and Africa is the mountain gorilla, found in rainforests (which are also under threat), and now on the verge of extinction. Rhinos, leopards, tigers and reptiles are also hunted. With so many of these species seemingly heading for extinction, usually due to human activity, we should not support exotic bloodsports.

Don't watch or support bullfights

Spanish, Portuguese and South American bullfights are controversial and bloody ways of celebrating life and death. Originating in Crete thousands of years ago, when they were seen as offerings to the gods, bullfights have now become simply a tourist sport. Every year many thousands of bulls and hundreds of horses are killed and maimed. Over $100 million is spent each year in tickets for Spanish bullfights, much of this money coming from tourists. When you go on holiday to countries where this activity is practised, do not support it.

Visit a national park

The vast national parks of Canada and the USA are often organized for the tourist, with camp sites, water taps, maps and scenic viewpoints. Some are left completely wild, and great care has to be taken before entering them. They often have fabulous wildlife and spectacular views. The national parks of the British Isles are also worth a visit, and offer hotels, holiday centres and bed-and-breakfast accommodation for short or long breaks.

On safari, don't run the animals into the ground

The delicate balance of water in the body of gazelles means that they can survive for long periods without adequate food and water in hot climates like Africa. When you come along in your jeep wanting to take photographs of these beautiful creatures you can inadvertently kill them. If you chase the animals to get your snap they exhaust themselves and often die on the spot. Safari holidays are questionable .on these grounds alone, and they need to be carefully managed to make sure that the holiday is not just another way of exploiting animals in the wild.

Conserve the skis

Skiing holidays have become another way for holiday-makers to become aware of the environment. Over the past few years, lack of snow on European slopes has meant that the US market has grown. The change might be due to global warming, but no one is quite sure just yet. It must be remembered that the skiing itself threatens and disrupts the ecological balance of the local area, however. Bird habitats have been depleted, deforestation across the mountainous Alp regions has further threatened wildlife and landslides have been more frequent because of lack of tree cover.

Canoe

Canoeing holidays are not for the fainthearted. They can be strenuous, but are exciting, and highly recommended. I was lucky enough to spend some time canoeing in Canada recently, and I saw more wildlife from the water than I had ever seen before. Canoes don't harm the environment – they've been used for hundreds of years by native Indians – and they are relatively safe and cheap. If you go camping and canoeing, be sure not to leave your rubbish around. Take it home with you and dispose of it carefully.

Have a cycling holiday

Not as strenuous as it sounds, a cycling holiday can consist of anything from day trips to long hauls. No pollution, no petrol, sheer person-power to get you around. Many holiday companies have cycling tours as options, but you can plan one yourself quite easily, with good maps and guide books.

Study while having fun

Try choosing a 'green' study holiday. Field-study groups, summer camps and courses offer a practical way to spend your free time and learn in the process. The idea of learning while having fun might seem strange to some people, but it can be more fun than you think. Environmental awareness, ecology and nature-study classes could be a wonderful way of discovering all the things you missed at school. You would meet like-minded people too.

Go remote

Remote cottages and cabins in wilderness areas offer great holidays for those who want to get away from it all. Nature and wildlife magazines often carry advertisements and you can walk, birdwatch and relax.

Go gourmet

International vegetarian handbooks can suggest ways of eating well while on holiday. Vegetarian meals can be found in almost every corner of the earth, so try alternatives.

Work on an organic farm

Working weekends on organic farms offer holidays with a difference. You can work your way to health! Spend time learning about organic farming, eating great food and generally being useful. It can be a positive break for city-dwellers.

Go walking

Forget the car! Go on a walking holiday. All across the world, walking holidays are becoming more popular. You can choose between mountains, hills, valleys and low-lying areas with footpaths. Walking saves energy, increases and stimulates good health and you can see much more from the road.

Go birdwatching

Birdwatching is one of the safest ways of admiring these beautiful creatures. Holiday specialists provide every possible comfort, and you can monitor birds for wildlife groups too, doing an important service. Too many birdwatchers can destroy the habitats of the very birds they have come to see, but most organized holidays are exceptionally careful.

Have a green Christmas break

At least one hotel in Britain offered a special green Christmas break during 1989/90, and after its success, there will no doubt be more in the coming years. A five-day break included vegetarian food, a visit to a nature reserve (as an alternative to the animal-hunting holidays of days gone by) and even a Santa in a green costume with fake fur!

Visit a city farm

City farms are springing up everywhere. London has five, and you can visit them as part of your urban break. They offer fantastic facilities for education and study groups, and are also great for day trips and interested armchair conservationists.

Don't take the roof-rack unless you need it

An unloaded roof-rack can increase your car's petrol consumption by nearly 10 per cent. If you need to use one for your holiday, then lay the largest suitcases flat, with smaller items packed at the back on top of each other. The load at the back should be higher than the front to get the best speed and petrol consumption.

Use organic insect repellents

When you go to a country with mosquitoes, midges or blackfly, oil of citronella is a good natural insect repellent. Non-organic commercial repellents contain diethyl toluamide (DEET), which is immediately poisonous if swallowed and has been responsible for many deaths. It is also absorbed through the skin when it is rubbed in, and tests show that repeated applications of a quite gentle solution can lead to brain disorders and effects on the central nervous system. Never use it over a long period. Unfortunately, the hotter you get, the more likely it is to be absorbed through your skin. I wouldn't recommend using DEET on children at all. A solution of vinegar can create a bad smell that wards off most insects. There are some new, commercially available, organic repellents, made with mixtures of essential oils that not only keep your skin supple but also create a nasty environment for insects. Where necessary, don't forget to take your malaria tablets!

Look out for a safer sunscreen

If you must sunbathe, then use a sunscreen. There are large

numbers of lotions and oils available that contain aloe vera, paba and cocoa butter, which are pleasant and comfortable to use. They are also often made now without animal-testing. But the only real way to protect yourself from harmful ultra-violet rays from the sun (which are now increasing in strength because of the thinning of the ozone layer) is not to sunbathe at all.

Make your time away a no-sunbathing holiday

The public are still generally unaware of the serious risks posed by sunbathing. Over 1,000 people died in Britain during 1987/88 from skin cancer; the numbers have doubled in just fifteen years. People most at risk are those who have a short sharp exposure to the sun in intensive sunbathing sessions on holiday. The ozone layer, over 24 kilometres (15 miles) above the earth, is thinning because of our use of CFCs and halons. The incidence of skin cancers will increase as the ozone layer becomes less and less able to screen out the sun's harmful ultra-violet rays. In countries such as Australia, where the number of skin-cancer deaths is enormous, government bodies are advising the general public to stay out of the sun.

Reject excessive packaging

You are more likely to come across restaurants that serve individually wrapped portions of butter, sugar, salt, pepper and ketchup while in aeroplanes, airports and holiday areas. Some countries insist that restaurants use these individual packages to cut down on possible food contamination, but there has been no clear evidence to show that contamination of foodstuffs is higher when you share a ketchup bottle with someone else, provided the restaurant is clean in the first place. Don't take condiments like sugar and salt unless you know you are going to use them. If you reject them immediately they are likely to be re-used instead of thrown away.

Beware 'photos ready in an hour'

The hour-processing-holiday-snap booths that operate in train stations and busy shopping precincts may not be environmentally friendly. They often don't have the facilities to recycle the chemicals used to develop the films. As a result, toxic chemicals such as silver, ferrocyanide and nitrates are added to the general waste stream. Next time you take a film to be developed, ask if the chemicals will be recycled. Use other facilities if the answer is no.

Camp CFC-free

Rigid and flexible foams, which are ozone destroyers, reach further than the supermarket shelves; they can end up in your camping gear too. Foam mattresses use chlorinated compounds that attack the ozone layer. Get yourself an inflatable-type mattress instead.

Camp on natural fibres

Synthetic fibres in your sleeping-bags aren't too comfortable to sleep in if it is hot out. The fibres don't absorb moisture very well, so you feel sticky and hot, and there is as well potential for an allergic reaction. The fibres are made from petrochemicals, which are heavy polluters, and you might be better off with a cotton sleeping-bag, or a cotton sheet next to your skin if you have already got a nylon sleeping-bag.

Duty free or a real duty?

Most people buy duty-free goods when they travel abroad. In Britain we spend 359 ECU (European Currency Unit = 1 ECU = £1) each per year on duty-free goods, mostly tobacco, alcohol and perfume. Duty-free goods are often the most wasteful in packaging of all the ways that we can buy these goods. They have boxes and layers of wrapping-paper inside, and plastic coverings as well as expensive gimmicks to sell them. If you are buying duty-free, don't buy all the wrapping too. Complain, hand the wrappings back before you leave, and send the inside packaging later. Ask the shops to cut down on the paper and plastic they use.

Take homoeopathic remedies on holiday

Special homoeopathic remedies are available for stomach upsets and diarrhoea – very important when you are on holiday. Don't waste time trying to block and unblock your system with extra chemicals. Use arsenicum album for food poisoning and vomiting or nux vomica for diarrhoea and upsets after too much rich food. Both are available from health food shops. Better still, eat wisely and moderately.

Don't take throwaways

It has become the fashion these days to take disposable wipes with us on holidays and days out. These are often drenched in perfumes and chemicals (which make my face spring out in blotches). They are also made from rayon, the origin of which is trees, and the manufacture causes much pollution: to delignify or break down the wood fibres, chlorine is used, which results in pollution from over 1,000 chemicals, including dioxins. I always take a cotton handkerchief – it is so easy to rinse it out!

Never dump plastics

Plastics are not biodegradable. They stay around in the environment forever, and one of the biggest threats to wildlife is the casual dumping of bags and other debris that can be eaten by birds and animals. Over 2 million seabirds and 100,000 sea mammals die every year from discarded plastics. Baby seals have been found strangled by plastic bags and discarded fishing nets; seabirds get caught in plastic ring-can holders, which are said to take 500 years to biodegrade; even whales have been washed ashore with up to fifty plastic bags inside their guts. The message is clear: don't dump plastics in the seas or on the road.

Eat local food

When you are away from home, do not rush to fast-food shops for dinner. Eat the food of the country you are in, and save resources. You will eat better, and more cheaply, too.

Stop the trade in endangered species

On exotic package-holidays in the Seychelles, East Africa and South America, North American and European tourists buy elephants' feet for wastepaper baskets; cowrie shells; tortoise-shells; coral and ivory trinkets. This souvenir trade is endangering species throughout the world. International law is difficult to enforce in all countries across the world, but it is up to you. Think carefully about the presents you bring home next time – it could be the end of the line for some species.

Refuse to have your photo taken with a chimp

Those cuddly-looking chimps found in Spanish resorts for you to be photographed with are caught in the wild. In West Africa, their mothers are shot and the baby chimps grabbed by poachers. To make them seem cuddly and calm they are often injected with drugs, then dressed in clothes and foisted on unsuspecting but delighted holiday-makers. They also can carry diseases that may be passed on to humans, including rabies and hepatitis, and as they are smuggled into the country they are not medically examined. Protect the chimpanzee; refuse this barbaric practice if you see it and report any photographers to the local authorities or to the World Wide Fund for Nature.

Don't bring back seeds and plants

When visiting a foreign country it is tempting to bring back a cutting of a particularly special plant or flower. Don't. It is probably illegal, and, even more important, you might also unwittingly bring back all sorts of tiny insects or bugs that could destroy your garden – or even your whole neighbour-hood. Respect other people's countryside, and leave it where it belongs.

Protect marine turtles

Marine turtles live in the sea but return to land to lay their eggs. That is when holiday-makers come into contact with them. The female lays her eggs on the beach, burying them up to 90 centimetres (35 inches) in the sand. After two months the baby turtles hatch and rush to the sea. They must reach the water quickly if they are not to be eaten by dogs, birds or crabs. Humans should stay away from these hatchlings, however fascinating they are.

Visit the whales – but with caution

Dolphins and killer whales have been captured and kept in dolphinaria for many years, giving delight to thousands of children and adults. But their average lifespan in captivity is only about five years; in the wild the killer whale can live to be eighty years old. If you want to see these beautiful mammals, the best and least harmful way is to visit them in their natural habitat. Visits can be arranged in California, Alaska and Norway. But note: the sheer volume of boat traffic from holiday-makers can cause problems for the whales as they are viewed in their breeding lagoons. If you must go, only go on boats with responsible tour operators. The most environmentally sound way to see these creatures is from viewing areas on land.

Don't walk on sand dunes

If you go to the beach this year you might see ridges of sand and grasses building up a few metres inland. These sand dunes are one of our most delicate habitats. They offer tenuous shelter for snakes and rare lizards such as the sand lizard. Natural erosion from the sea forms ponds where natterjack toads mate. Many species of plant and grasses line miles of ridges that hold thousands of amphibians. It might take up to a hundred years to form a single ridge, but it takes only one hot summer season for the public to walk or drive over it and destroy it completely. Walk only on boardwalks. If there aren't any, complain and campaign for them. Walk on established walkways and never, never drive cars over the paths.

Stop persecuting snakes!

There is an ancient myth, probably originating in the Bible, that snakes are dangerous. Snakes are not protected in the wild, and when the public see them they often kill them in fear. Stop! They are just not as dangerous as you think. Even adders aren't lethal, and they will not attack if left alone. Snakes need an open habitat in the sun in order to live, being cold-blooded creatures, and so they risk being spotted during the day. All reptiles have fixed territories and snakes are no exception. This means that when their habitat is destroyed, they don't recolonize somewhere else – they just die out. Next time you see a snake, respect it and don't kill it or disturb its habitat – it may be the last one.

The Countryside

Visit the countryside

At least 25 per cent of city dwellers have never been to the countryside at all, and yet a visit offers so much in terms of fresh air, country walks and a different view of the world. Support your countryside, and visit it as often as you can.

Observe the countryside code

The British Countryside Commission has published a code for visitors to the countryside. Green visitors should be aware of all its recommendations.

 1. Enjoy the countryside and respect its life and work
 2. Guard against all risks of fire
 3. Fasten all gates
 4. Keep your dogs under close control
 5. Use gates and stiles to cross fences, hedges and walls
 6. Leave livestock, crops and machinery alone
 7. Keep to the public paths across farmland
 8. Take your litter home
 9. Help to keep all water clean
10. Protect wildlife, plants and trees
11. Take special care on country roads
12. Make no unnecessary noise

Observe the farmer's code

Faith Sharp of the *Countryman* magazine has devised a code for farmers in the countryside. Her advice may be of interest to all green visitors to the country as well.

1. Respect those who come to enjoy the countryside and make them welcome
2. Guard against damage to trees and hedges caused by straw-burning
3. Make sure that gates on public paths are in good order and easy to open
4. Keep bulls out of fields that have rights of way
5. Reinstate public paths across fields immediately after ploughing, and never plough headland paths
6. Don't use barbed wire where paths cross
7. Don't remove or twist around signposts, or put 'Private' notices where there is a right of way
8. Take old fertilizer bags home with you
9. Don't pollute watercourses, ponds and lakes with farm sprays or effluents
10. Don't destroy wildlife by indiscriminate ploughing, hedge-clearing, draining or pond-filling
11. Avoid damaging verges and wildlife with heavy farm machinery
12. Don't shout at walkers in your corn. They are probably on the right of way you have planted over

Never drop litter in the countryside

Litter in the countryside is a double trap. Plastic is not biodegradable, and it can also kill small mammals and birds.

If you go to the countryside, please take your litter home with you when you return. Don't feed wild animals and don't leave food behind at picnic sites and camping grounds, however tempting it seems.

Don't take cars into wildlife areas

During the summer of 1989, police in the Lake District had to close the area, as the number of cars caused a huge traffic jam. Use your car only when you need to. Try walking more than the average thirty paces from the car into the country and you might see more than you expect.

Never climb walls

Dry-stone walls are vulnerable to the weather and human influence if they are not properly maintained. They can easily crumble and fall into disrepair: they become eyesores and sheltering animals lose their homes. Climbing walls accelerates deterioration. Never take stones from walls for the garden.

Close gates and fences

A golden rule that farmers always observe is to close gates. It sounds simple enough, but if it is not done it can allow farm animals into roads, where they can reach other fields, destroy crops and cause havoc.

Don't dump your car

Cars dumped in countryside areas are monumental eyesores. They should be disposed of carefully and with thought to the environment and the local landscape. Don't dump or abandon your car, and report those who do to the local authorities.

Save our orchards

Conserving, saving and planting orchards is not only an important part of our heritage, but maintains diversity and habitats for wildlife. Orchards are havens for wild flowers, bees and birds. And life around a fruit orchard can be rich and varied. You can have tastings and sales of old, unusual varieties of fruit; 'apple' teas; cookery demonstrations; competitions; cider and perry tastings; and damson-jam sales and apple roadshows. Orchards also make perfect grazing for cattle, sheep, pigs and poultry, and are valued for walking and relaxing.

Replant hedgerows

Between 1980 and 1985 some 37,600 kilometres (22,560 miles) of hedgerows were removed in Britain, and only 4,025 kilometres (2,415 miles) were replanted. Some of the hedges dated back over three hundred years. The oldest documented hedgerow was flourishing in Northumberland in AD 547. Hedgerows protect animal herds, act as stopping points for birds, mammals and insects and are a refuge for wildlife. They also keep soil within a boundary, so that it is not blown away by the wind. Over 250 species of wild flower have been recorded around hedgerows, but all are now sadly under great pressure. New financial incentives for farmers may help stop the loss. Contact conservation groups who can help with replanting.

Curb the spread of Rhododendron ponticum

The purple *Rhododendron ponticum* is an invasive plant. It is a native of Turkey and was brought to the British Isles in the late eighteenth-century. It is now colonizing much of Britain, spreading from gardens and estates. Its growth speed is phenomenal: 10.000 seeds weigh only 1 gram and are quickly dispersed by even light winds. Over 1 per cent of Snowdonia National Park in Wales is covered by *rhododendron ponticum*. The bush does not support any insect life, prevents woodland regeneration, is poisonous to mammals and produces an acid humus that stops regrowth even if the plant is removed.

If you want to protect it, buy it!

Conservation groups can protect land and buildings by buying them. Successful campaigns have been won by groups like Friends of the Earth in Oxford, which purchased from a local farmer a field that was due to be developed into part of a new motorway. They then divided up the land into smaller plots and sold them, so a compulsory purchase order for the land would have meant summonsing literally thousands of landowners for just one tiny field. The group managed to raise awareness about the flora and fauna found in the field as well as question the need for the motorway. Organizations around the world buy land for protection and campaigning – why not support them?

Create a habitat

New habitats can be created, and this goes some way to making up for the tragic loss of meadows and wildflower and woodland copses in the past twenty years. The habitats need to be managed properly if they are to survive, and many conservation groups and nature trusts have information and experience on their side. If you know of a derelict area or a piece of land that could be planted, start some action. Don't let it go to waste.

Support our woodlands

Growing mixes of trees native to our country help support

our woodlands. But over two-thirds of British woodland are now conifer plantations for paper-making or pulping. Many of them have been grown for tax advantages alone, and yet ancient, deciduous woodlands are the most valuable of our wildlife habitats. More species of birds are associated with woodlands than anywhere else, and they hold a rich and diverse variety of plants and animals. Cut down on your paper use and support charities and organizations that plant new trees in woodlands and protect those already standing.

Plant what's best for the wild

Planting Sitka spruce and Corsican pine does not help the environment much just because they are trees. Native evergreens or other species live longer and support more wildlife species. A single oak, for example, can be a home for 284 species alone – and they are less prone to diseases. Planting native hardwood trees should be a priority. Campaign against those who plant imported varieties for pulping, for tax or for other financial advantages.

Campaign against drainage

Every important wetland site in Britain is threatened by proposed drainage schemes. Draining wetlands has long been the policy of farmers, aided and abetted by generous grants from the Ministry of Agriculture. Some of our most important wildlife sites, especially bird sites, have been irreversibly destroyed. If you live in a farming community you could help by lobbying locally elected representatives. Everyone, in every community, should be aware that draining wetlands for peat extraction is destroying much of our ancient wildlife habitat.

Save the forests

Our own forests are in danger, not just the rainforests in

Brazil and other tropical places. At least half of all British woodlands have been destroyed in the last forty years, and many species of animals and plants have become rare or extinct because of their loss. The heath fritillary butterfly abounded in at least fifty sites some years ago, but today it can only be found in six sites. Species like nuthatches, woodpeckers and nightingales depend on the forests for their survival. Conifer planting has destroyed land and species and is not the answer to our once-rich forests. Support groups that replant and look after forest areas, especially local forests and woodland areas.

Conserve the meadows

There are so very few meadowlands left to conserve that we should do all we can to preserve them. Centuries ago meadowland was unrestricted, mostly commonland and grazing space. With intensive farming much of our meadowland has been lost. We no longer leave a field fallow every four years so it can enrich itself with wildflowers, providing a good compost for the following years' crop. About 25 per cent of meadow plants are grasses. The rest consists of wild flowers like the meadow clary, cuckoo flower or marsh marigold. Meadow plants thrive in poor soil and grazing animals on fallow fields helped create many of our ancient and beautiful meadows. You can help conserve meadows by campaigning against development on those remaining, and joining and supporting groups who work on conservation projects.

Replant free food

Blackberries, elderflowers and soft-fruit bushes should be planted in country areas to reintroduce free food for humans and wildlife. The British elderflower once made legendary wine, but with the loss of so many hedgerows, and chemical

sprays on what is left, these bushes are few and far between. Plant bushes and trees yourself, encourage farmers and local councils to do so.

Support wildlife sanctuaries

Wildlife sanctuaries allow a safe refuge for all wild animals and plants from hunters and collectors. So far 1,000 hectares (2,500 acres) of the most beautiful countryside in Britain have been set aside for herds of red deer, precious wildflower meadows, ancient woodlands and wetlands. Sensitive wildlife management can encourage and enhance local ecology. You can support groups setting up or managing wildlife sanctuaries by joining them or visiting.

Protect rural verges

Britain's major and minor roads account for an incredible 200,000 hectares (500,000 acres) of land. The roadside verges contain a mass of wildflower species, mammals, birds and insects. Spraying and clearing these verges destroys much of the potential habitat. You can help to protect verges by not throwing litter, asking local authorities to let the wild flowers grow (this would even save them money) and asking local naturalist or wildlife groups to carry out surveys for monitoring and protection.

Curtail military and development activities in protected areas

The development of intensive farming, upland farming, fish farming, commercial building, and military activities are putting extra strain on the already small areas of land protected to enhance and preserve the natural beauty of a given area. All the main countryside and protection organizations have asked for a curtailment of further development on these sites.

Support the small farmer

The 'holistic' approach of organic agriculture encompasses balance, health and wholeness as its central principles. Organic food is superior in quality and taste to chemically produced food, and using and re-using resources means that nothing is wasted. Rotation farming keeps the soil in good condition, and with the right amount of nutrients the organic farmer will show a higher yield over time. Intensive farming on a large scale means less work for farmers. This increases the number of unemployed, brings more pollution from pesticides and creates a demand for high energy. Small farms employ more person power and less chemical and mechanical help. You can support small farms and organic farming by buying organically produced food.

Campaign against crop spraying

Friends of the Earth have recorded thousands of accidents that involve farmers who spray large areas of crops. Many members of the public have been poisoned. Cases have included pregnant women losing babies and small children becoming suddenly ill.

Support the use of straw

Although a three-year moratorium has been placed on straw- and stubble-burning in Britain, it does not cover all crops, and in any case expires in 1992. Straw-burning causes serious environmental problems – not just the danger of air pollution and smoke, but also the lost use of the straw as a resource in itself. Part of the reason it is burned is that it is too cheap to merit transportation, but animals that used to be bedded on straw are now housed on concrete slats. And straw and animal litter mix which used to be used as compost has now been swapped for a peat mix. This is increasing the rate of destruction of our peat boglands. But mixing animal waste and even domestic sewage with straw means that an inexpensive alternative is available to peat. Buying straw-based papers has also increased the market for straw. Buying only humanely reared meat products would encourage farmers to stop straw-burning and start seeing straw as a useful resource again.

Take the land out of agriculture

Land in the countryside does not need to be used continuously for growing crops. It is beneficial for the environment to increase the amount of land that is set aside for wildlife to flourish, for recreational facilities and for conservation projects like nature reserves. Less intensive farming and less intensive livestock management helps. This means that we should have to eat lower down the food table, instead of relying so much on meat and meat-based products. The massive food surplus that we have in Britain can be reversed and land could be left to allow flora and fauna to flourish.

Ban aerial spraying

Aerial spraying of crops with pesticides must be the most wasteful and ecologically damaging of all intensive agricultural methods. Several surveys show that only 5 per cent of the chemicals reached the intended pests. Small farmers do not generally need to use planes for crop spraying, but the larger, commercially orientated farms cut down the hedges and make huge strips of land which are then ready for bigger machines and more mechanized forms of farming. Friends of the Earth have monitored human and animal accidents due to haphazard pesticide spraying and have recommended a ban. If you live in the country, you should report all incidences of crop spraying to the local authorities and your Environmental Health Officer as a public nuisance. Protect yourself by never getting in the way of sprays and report to a doctor if you should be sprayed accidentally. Eat organically produced food.

Don't confine pregnant animals

Inhumane practices in intensive farming mean that we rear pregnant animals in cruel conditions. Sows can be kept in tiny stalls, unable to move or lie properly. This practice should not continue, and ending it is unlikely to harm the farmer one bit. Write to your supermarket and ask if it condones this sort of practice. Don't buy from companies that appear to support such cruelty.

Campaign against lamping the badger

The latest craze in countryside sports is lamping badgers. On late autumn evenings and early in the morning badgers look for earthworms on exposed newly ploughed fields, and this is where the badger-baiters wait. The baiters use lamps to blind the badgers, and then the dogs are set on them, mauling them to death. Numbers of badgers have declined in farming areas in the UK, mostly because of the lack of hedgerows. Also, many badgers were gassed some years ago because of fears that they could spread the TB virus to cows. Now they are protected. Badgers live in a complex series of tunnels in a set, and they annoy farmers because they construct breather holes along their routes, generally in the middle of fields. Baiting and lamping these creatures is a cruel sport and not a good way to protect farming land.

Cull deer by shooting, not stag-hunting

Deer, Britain's largest wild animals, are hunted by experienced hounds, chased to exhaustion and then shot by the riders. Female hinds may well be pregnant, or have calves with them, which may also be savaged by the hounds. Teeth, feet and antlers are often sold as souvenirs. The stag-hunters hunt the strong deer, not the weak, old or lame animals – so they can't ever use deer control or culling as justification. Years ago wild predators such as wolves would have selected and killed deer, as part of the natural ecosystem. Culling deer by shooting is a more efficient and less cruel way to keep numbers down in the countryside.

Make snares illegal

Approximately one-third of the animals caught in snares are actually targeted species. Other animals mistakenly trapped include cats, dogs, badgers, deer, hedgehogs and partridges. It is illegal to set snares for some animals, like deer or badgers, and the 1981 Wildlife and Countryside Act outlawed the self-locking snare and states that 'reasonable precautions must be taken to prevent injury to protected animals'. The RSPCA (Royal Society for the Prevention of Cruelty to Animals) believes that as snares do not discriminate between species this is impossible to maintain, and it wants to make all snares illegal. Support groups that are campaigning to get all snares banned, and don't set them yourself.

Bring back the red squirrel

Lowland Britain has lost its population of red squirrels, not because the grey squirrels have pushed it out, as is commonly thought, but because of the massive loss of woodland tree cover. This is now only between 7 and 9 per cent of the total land area, the lowest in Europe. The infectious diseases mange and coccidiosis are also thought to be partly responsible. Unlike grey squirrels, red squirrels have not been able to adapt to urban areas. By planting more woodland in country areas we may help bring back the red squirrel.

Build hedgehog crossings on cattle grids

Many small animals such as hedgehogs find it impossible to get out of the steep pits that make up cattle or sheep grids. These grids are death traps. A small ramp or slope in one corner of the pit would enable them to walk to freedom.

Protect the owl

The most common bird of prey in Britain is the owl, which feeds on a diet of mice, rats and voles. Every single type of owl is now under threat in the countryside. Our use of pesticides and chemicals on farms and our poisoning of their food has helped in the massive decline in the numbers of these nocturnal creatures that have perfect hearing and silent flight. We still know very little about them. Only 135 species exist, and most of them are now rare, so do all you can to protect them. Monitor them, report them (dead or alive), put up nesting boxes and allow rodents to breed without chemical poisoning in the countryside.

Don't dig up wild plants

Increasing pressure from industrial and housing developments, agriculture and forestry, threatens natural habitats. Over 300 of Britain's 1,500 known plant species are threatened with extinction. Legislation gives some protection to Britain's hundred rarest plants, but the public can also play a role in saving them. On country walks many people might feel tempted to pick wildflowers or to dig up bulbs to take home to their gardens. Please leave them for everyone to enjoy.

Protect the orchid

Fourteen of Britain's forty orchid species are thought to be threatened almost to extinction in the countryside, and the rest are becoming increasingly rare because of their special and laborious flowering. It can take up to fifteen years for an orchid to flower after germination, and destruction of downland, changes in woodland management and the drainage of wetlands have all led to the loss of orchids in the wild. The theft of wild orchid seeds is a serious conservation problem.

Protect birds' eggs

Birds' eggs found in the wild can often be valuable for unscrupulous traders. But never touch eggs if you find them. If you think they are particularly rare, contact the local birdwatchers' association, who can monitor them safely.

Save the natterjack toad

A rare toad indeed: the natterjack is the rarest amphibian in Britain. It can only be saved by increasing the numbers of nature reserves and protecting sites of ecological importance, like sand dunes. Supporting groups financially, lobbying and campaigning for protected areas are the only ways of preserving the habitats of this unusual creature.

Protect the otter

The otter must be one of Britain's favourite water mammals, and yet its life is threatened by our pollution. It may already be too late to save the otter, as the spread of intensive farming has destroyed its lowland habitat. Support groups like the Otter Trust, who designate otter havens. If you are in a position to do so, then plant thickets, willows and other undergrowth along streams and water banks to give otters the chance to hide in the relative safety of the banks where they once used to thrive.

Keep to footpaths

Several thousands of miles of footpaths in Britain, Europe and America are favourite destinations for wildlife enthusiasts, ramblers and hikers. Keep to the footpaths when you walk across farmland and do not spoil the crops or frighten the animals.

Protect your footpaths

An environmental disaster is looming for hill and dale walkers, who use the same footpaths so often. The Pennine Way, in the Peak District, is an example. The favourite walk there is over 90 metres (100 yards) wide in places from the pressure of hikers' boots. If you are on a footpath with muddy places, go through the mud rather than trying to edge around it, which only creates a wider path.

Campaign for more footpaths

More footpaths would take the pressure off some of the more popular paths and would add new scenic and adventurous walks for hikers and ramblers. Ask your nearest national park to create more footpaths.

Coppice and pollard in woodlands

Coppicing and pollarding bushes and small trees is an ancient practice. It ensures that trees are left enough space for some to grow to maturity and others, especially trees like hazels and limes, to produce a secondary layer of light and shade. This is great for wildlife, and provides extra wood for fuel, fencing and a wide variety of other purposes.

Improve rural bus services

In the past few years deregulation of rural bus services in Britain has meant that local people in some areas have had to live without adequate means of transportation. For many this means resorting to their cars to get them out of their homes, for others who cannot afford to drive, or do not want to, it means seclusion and loneliness. Deregulating buses means fewer and fewer services operate in areas not considered profitable. As the numbers of cars increase so does pollution, consumption of petrol and the number of road accidents.

Support your village shop

Village shops and post offices are lifelines for local communities, particularly for old people. Many shops find it difficult to survive, however, when local residents go speeding off in their new cars to buy supplies from supermarkets often many miles away. The supermarket goods may be cheaper, but people usually forget to add in the cost of travelling to the supermarket and parking the car, as well as the extra pollution caused and the time wasted in travelling. Support local village shops wherever you can; they are good news for the environment.

Use the river network

River networks around the world offer much loved forms of transport: barges in Holland, gondolas in Italy and junks in China all conjure up romantic and beautiful images. On a practical level the river network offers a mode of transport that could have repercussions for our future transportation plans. Imagine transporting goods along the rivers on barges instead of in heavy lorries or increasing the number of people who could use the Thames to get to work. If you can, why not use the river network and take pressure off the roads?

Put up signs

Farmers, landowners, conservation groups and local councils should work together to ensure the protection of our countryside. Signs for the public can make all the difference between knowledge and ignorance. Instead of 'Beware!' why not try 'Stop! Save our natural habitats from extinction'? Protection of plant and animal species might be easier for the public with a more positive approach.

The Green Citizen

Local Community

Work with animals

Make a positive commitment to wildlife and the environment by joining the thousands of people working to save, protect and look after animals. Kennel or stable work, farming and veterinary surgery are just some of the worthwhile careers available.

Plant a tree

We do know that the planting of trees is generally beneficial. Trees enhance their surroundings, provide a home and shade for wildlife and birds, and soak up carbon dioxide. But you should always think carefully before planting. Almost 50 per cent of trees planted die within a few years because they are not chosen for the type of soil carefully enough or they are not looked after properly. By looking after existing trees and encouraging natural germination you may reduce the need to plant in country areas. By choosing good varieties with care, you can ensure that trees planted will survive.

Never write off trees

After the storm of October 1987, in the South of England, more trees were damaged and killed by well-meaning helpers quickly 'clearing-up' than by the storm itself. A tree can often survive with only one quarter of its roots left. Dead wood even adds beauty to an area and protection for wildlife and recycles nutrients back into the soil. If you have the choice, it's better to leave dead trees where they are.

Start a tree register

Be a detective! Record the trees in your local parish, in roads, courtyards, orchards, hedgerows and churches. You can trace the origins of certain fruit trees. Every Bramley apple tree in Britain can be traced back to one magnificent old tree in Nottinghamshire that is 170 years old. Identify those trees that are local landmarks or mark boundaries.

Create a milestone

Encourage a whole new generation of environmental art in your community. Stimulate the creation of small-scale art works to express your sense of love of the natural world and its history. You can create new landmarks and new beginnings. Be proud of your place in the community.

Use the bottle bank

There are 17,000 people for every bottle bank in Britain, and some 70 local authorities do not operate schemes at all. In countries like Holland, 62 per cent of glass is recycled due to the efficient bottle-bank system. In Toronto, Canada, glass is now picked up every week at the doorstep. Until we have enforceable laws governing collections of glass for recycling it is better for the environment to take bottles, rinsed clean, to your nearest bottle bank. We need one bottle bank for every 2,000 people for effective recycling, so campaign within your local council to get this enforced.

Organize a parish map

The British organization, Common Ground, has been encouraging local communities to collaborate on parish map projects. Local people, or even a commissioned artist, can draw or sew the things that they value and respect on an illustrated map. Parish councils, schools, women's institutes, local history or environment groups can join together to chart and map the things that are valued in each community. Over 500 maps have already been started in Britain, from David Nash's 'Personal Parish' in Ffestiniog, Wales, represented only in words, to Pat John's 'Topsham Observance' tapestry, reflecting hidden values in past and present life.

Protect trees

Cutting down a tree should be a last resort. Their importance as spiritual, cultural and emotional companions is only just being rediscovered. Many trees are protected by law already and it is illegal to fell them; more protection orders should be granted. Before we cut down a single tree we should consider the wildlife that depends on it, whether the timber is to be put to a worthwhile use and whether other trees will be allowed to grow and replace it.

Don't always burn your autumn leaves

Leaves on the streets can be dangerous and slippery, but the efficiency of local authorities who clear away leaves in urban areas can upset the ecological balance of insects like wasps, moths and flies. The recent epidemic of the scale insect on urban sycamore and horse chestnut is thought to be due to the hurried burning of its predator, the chalcid wasp, which stays fixed to the underside of fallen dead leaves during autumn. Over 400 types of leaf-mining moths live on the underside of dead leaves alone and the caterpillar, greenfly and hopperfly all pupate in the leaf and meet an early death if burnt. A better alternative is to compost the leaves, thereby keeping the streets clear while allowing natural biological control and making a rich organic mix for use on parks and gardens.

Leave some dog-free areas

Not everyone likes dogs; they can upset children and wildlife and one of the biggest environmental problems identified by the public in opinion polls is dog faeces. By declaring some park and wildlife areas 'dog-free' you will be enhancing the community and environment. The parasites in dog faeces can cause serious illnesses, even blindness, in young children who touch it, so do not allow dogs to defecate in children's areas.

Encourage Buddleia for butterflies on wasteland

The *Buddleia davidii* is now a common shrub in north London waste sites. It can grow easily in very poor soil and the carbon dioxide from its roots forms an acidic solution to dissolve spaces in walls for it to establish itself. This plant is particularly attractive to butterflies, especially the Peacock, Small Tortoiseshell, Red Admiral and Painted Lady.

Complain about the state of your pavement

Bad footpaths cause an astonishing number of accidents; at least 200 people die each year walking on the road and pavements. Regular walking in your local area will help you notice what is going on around you. Complain to your local council about the state of paths and pedestrian walkways. This will keep it on its toes and contribute to safety.

Use your motorcycle with consideration

An annoying form of environmental pollution is noise. Noisy motorbikes outside your window at 1 a.m. can be very aggravating. A noisy motorbike is said to be able to wake thousands of people late at night so if you use one, be considerate. Getting the law changed to tighten exhaust/silencer controls would also help. If someone has removed or altered a motorcycle silencer, you can prosecute through your local environmental health officer, who will need to test the offending motorbike. Many motorbikes can run on lead-free petrol without conversion – ask your dealer.

Ban heavy lorries

Heavy lorries are a menace. British lorries are allowed to carry 38 tonnes. They cause damage to the environment, break up road surfaces, cause heavy wear on bridges such as the Severn Bridge and enormous damage to the underground cables and pipes in cities like London. The Swiss have unilaterally banned all lorries over 28 tonnes and have stopped all-night lorry driving. Combined rail and road options are a more environmentally friendly and cost-effective way of transporting freight. By banning heavy lorries in your area you will be able to force the government and large companies to use the rail system to transport goods, reducing pollution and havoc.

Don't support incineration of rubbish

Some people think that the incineration of rubbish, to obtain extra energy and to dispose of our rubbish mountains, is good for the environment and is a new energy source. But evidence is mounting that the incineration of mixed rubbish is not only dangerous but economically unviable. Large waste-incinerators release dangerous gases into the air, including dioxins, and certain mixtures of waste create hydrochloric acid, cadmium, lead, mercury and selenium. Yet if we really recycled to our maximum potential we would only have 4 per cent of the rubbish that we have now to be disposed of, which would be economically unviable to incinerate. Municipal incinerators are a major source of dangerous dioxins in our environment.

Investigate weed-killers in your street

If you see local authority workers spraying grass verges and streets with weed-killers, you have every right to ask them what chemicals they are using and why. A growing number of local councils are stopping the use of chemical weed-killers like those containing atrazine and simazine. Evidence suggests that these chemicals are endangering wildlife and contaminating drinking water. A Surrey council inquiry found dead birds near the spraying sites a few weeks after contractors sprayed the chemicals. Laboratory evidence suggests that the chemicals are irritants and could cause severe allergic reactions. Atrazine can damage various organs and is a suspected carcinogen. Workers are increasingly demanding better safety checks on such herbicides, and some councils, like Colchester in Essex, have agreed to use them only as a last resort.

Watch out for sea-dumping

The sea is often thought of as the perfect place to dump unwanted wastes like sewage and toxic chemicals. Pesticides have been burnt at sea for twenty years. Toxic wastes can be simply thrown overboard in drums. The risks to aquatic life are considerable. It is now estimated that over 100,000 different chemicals are in the North Sea alone. Drums of toxic waste that are illegally thrown overboard can be washed up on to beaches, and leaking drums cause serious pollution. If you spot suspicious drums on local beaches, report them to your local water authority immediately.

Take your hands off city walls

Graffiti make your local environment look a mess. They are illegal and dangerous. Most so-called artists use aerosol cans, which not only damage the ozone layer or contribute to global warming but also eject tiny particles of toxic paint substances, including glues, which can be addictive and hazardous. It costs local government and companies literally millions to remove graffiti from walls, trains, buses and shops.

Join a group

There are millions of people around the world campaigning to save the planet. They come from all walks of life, and you could be one of them. Read the newspapers, get hold of books and magazines, join an environmental group – or form one – and support those who are spending time doing research and campaigning about some of the important issues raised in this guide.

Don't drop litter

Litter costs your community money and destroys your local environment. If you decide to drop rubbish all around your house, you can continue to do so in privacy, but you should never do so in public. Get into the habit of telling people that you find dropping litter unacceptable. If enough people complained, it certainly might discourage one or two litter louts. Don't forget that wildlife also suffers when you drop litter. Birds can choke on plastic and small mammals can get very sick and even die because of rubbish left around when they are hungry. Litter also attracts and encourages rats and mice.

Support candidates who run on environmental platforms

Vote for those people who you know understand, and will carry out, good environmental policies. Ask them questions about what they will do for you in office, get commitments and get them to stick to them if they are elected.

Write letters to elected representatives

Whether you voted for them or not, local and national politicians are responsible to you, the public. If you write to them protesting about a particular matter they will have to take note. The size of the postbag really does influence elected officials.

Report illegal dumping

Be a super-snoop! Illegal dumping is on the increase, by industry as well as individuals. Dumping rubbish can be extremely dangerous, both to children and wildlife, and the proliferation of unmanned waste tips, often in residential areas, is an eyesore. If you see dumpers, don't hesitate to call your local authority or police.

Complain about litter-bins

If your local shops, take-away restaurants and council aren't providing litter-bins, you should complain until they do. Litter with nowhere to go ends up on the pavement.

Do a wildlife and buildings survey

Examine the types of building, landscape and animal habitat in your area. This will give you scope and inspiration for action to protect or enhance them.

Get other groups involved

Looking after the environment is not just for conservation and nature groups. Ask the local Guides and Scouts to help, or the local community centre, over-65 club or citizens' action committee. Getting other people involved spreads the message and the workload.

Look after your playing fields

The long stretches of grass in playing fields offer a haven for migratory birds and seabirds. A set-aside area could be encouraged to grow wild flowers and attract butterflies and other wildlife.

Look after churchyards and cemeteries

Churchyards and cemeteries in rural areas may have escaped pesticide poisoning altogether and may be sanctuaries for all kinds of wildlife. Some cemeteries are so rich in ecological diversity that they have been turned into nature reserves. Protect them whenever you can. Record the nature and state of trees and the number of plants and shrubs. Don't let them be destroyed, make sure your local council or church group knows how precious they are.

Look after your local waterways

Improve and protect your local waterways. They are a valuable home for wildlife and all manner of plants and flowers. Local conservation groups are involved with clean-up operations and restoring such areas to their natural beauty. They can be a perfect escape in an urban area and riverbanks, waterways and canals make your local environment green and pleasant.

Repair it

Repair, replace, repaint. Broken railings and fences, badly maintained flower-beds and tumbledown walls will not improve your environment. Do something about it! Get together with people in your street or town. Ask for help from authorities and conservation groups. Once you notice what is happening you can set aside one or two days and do something really practical to help.

Get it sponsored

Activities like cleaning and clearing up your local environment can be combined with fundraising activities for local

charities and environment groups. Help them to help you.
Next time you are doing something active in your local
community, get it sponsored.

Look after bus shelters

Many bus shelters are eyesores unless looked after properly.
Painting, cleaning up graffiti and disposing of leaves and
rubbish are some of the important tasks that need to be
done regularly. Ask your local authority to help, or do it
yourself.

Protect your buildings

Some local buildings are an eyesore, but some are historic
and valuable monuments. Some have trees and grounds
which may not have been touched for many years. Historic
buildings societies and groups can monitor and pressurize
local officials to look after old buildings. Keep notes and
photographs, and offer solutions, designs and ideas for their
use.

Find a use for a building

Look out for under-used buildings in your community. Could
they be transformed into a home, space for a youth club, a
tenants' association office or a community centre? Get in
touch with the owners or the local authority and start something happening.

Adopt a roundabout

Adopt a local piece of land, like a traffic roundabout or green
square. Get permission to plant wild flowers, shrubs, bulbs,
even trees. Agree a plan for maintenance in advance and
make your area look greener.

Glorify your town square

Your town square is not going to be Trafalgar Square, but it can look great with a few improvements. Restore clocks and protect trees. Repaint seats and repair dustbins and walls. Take a photograph before and after and display them in your local library.

Start a footpath maintenance scheme

Maintain footpaths. Erect good signposts and mend stiles and gates. Clear vegetation and fallen trees if necessary and get help to maintain the surface of the path.

Plan in favour of women

Women are often the last to be thought of when it comes to local environments. Planning applications should be opposed unless they consider the needs of women and women with children, as well as disabled people. Dark streets, badly maintained walkways and poor access into shops and up stairs for mothers with pushchairs all show a local environment that is unfriendly and inconsiderate. You can have a say. Tell them what you want to see, influence your local decision-making process.

Fence with brambles and roses

Instead of barbed wire and broken glass, why not encourage brambles and wandering roses to do the job for you? They are much prettier, deter cats (and people) and will not harm birds.

Attend annual meetings

Go to the annual meetings of your local parish council, civic trust and other organizations. Find out what has been happening, and keep in touch. Even if you cannot always attend regularly, it should not be too difficult to get to an annual meeting.

Get a skip

If there is a lot of rubbish in your street, such as thrown-out sofas, old fires and furniture that cannot be re-used, call in a skip and get everyone to use it one Saturday. Get rid of unsightly and dirty garbage which attracts rats and makes your street look awful.

Use the public library

What better way to recycle books, use community facilities and read about the environment? Use your local library.

Plant flowers on your windowsill

If you do not have a garden, or you live in a flat, you can still encourage butterflies and birds and make your home look greener. Window-boxes can be filled with bulbs for spring and delicate summer flowers or herbs for later in the year.

Campaign for parking-spaces for cyclists

Bicycles take up almost no space at all, especially when compared to a car. They are free of pollutants and do not use precious energy. A real problem for city cyclists is the lack of safe places for parking. Why not ask your local shops, library, community centre or workplace to make sure that cycle sheds, cycle rungs or suitable parking-spaces are provided?

Hold an exhibition

Hold an exhibition. Show past and present community lifestyles, encourage others to join and be proud of their landscape, buildings and heritage.

Twin your town

Twin your town and encourage community spirit and co-operation with another country. Learn to live together, and learn about how others live. Share ideas and resources.

Hold a competition

Provide the community with some fun. Hold a photography competition to spot the best wildlife in your area; or the best-kept street or avenue. Ask local businesses to donate prizes and get the local paper involved. Get people thinking about their community.

Protect your landscape

Over 1 million acres of land have been concreted over in Britain in the last half-century, stripping our landscape of woodlands, trees, meadows and fields. Check all the planning applications you see in local papers or pinned to walls and trees. Get involved and interested in what developers are doing to your area. You have a say and you could save some valuable heritage from poor development planning.

Clean up your beaches

Join a group or contact your local authority and clean up unsightly waste from your beach or coastal area. This will not just benefit you, but also birds and marine life that live on the beaches and would probably appreciate a cleaner home.

Residential Hazards

Heavy lorries, exhaust fumes, loose paving stones, lack of safe places for kids to play, poor street lighting, muggers, dogs and what they leave behind.... How long do you want this list to be?

Be vigilant

Always be vigilant. Be aware that people, authorities and industries want to make changes all the time to planning controls, buildings and land. Obviously not every change is bad, some could even be beneficial to the environment, but constant vigilance is necessary in your area. Keep an eye on a certain area such as the walk to the bus or tube each morning on your way to work or school. Be alert to changes.

Clean up the landfill

Landfill sites are pretty noxious – after all, they hold millions of tonnes of our waste – but they can offer a haven to wildlife. Over the years, as better recycling facilities are organized, we should need fewer landfill sites, but schemes can help areas that have already been filled. One successful scheme already exists in England: a landfill site has been turned into a public park. The site was covered over with 45 centimetres (18 inches) of topsoil to contain the various gases and other by-products of rotting waste. Within five years, over 145 different species of wild plant were recovered in the area.

Inspect rivers and streams for pollution

Keep your eye open for dirty water. It might be coming from local businesses and sewers that are putting chemicals into the waste stream. Watch out for dead or dying fish and wildlife. They can be the first signs of hidden pollution. Notice which wild flowers, shrubs and bushes are doing well. Some like acidic soil better than others, and a keen gardener will be able to spot changes in soil and water conditions. Report any changes that worry you to local authorities immediately, making sure that they are aware of your concern. It might encourage them to improve their own monitoring. Never think that someone else will do it; they won't.

Grow flowers everywhere

Flowers make a community look like a home. They add colour and interest and their nectar attracts butterflies and bees. Get local garden-shops to donate bulbs for hospitals and schools. Make sure local businesses have tubs or window-boxes if they haven't got a green space. Let flowers cheer people up all year.

Find out who matters

Who owns you? Whom do you pay money to? Who represents

you in local elections? It is important that you know how your local community works. Be a sleuth, ask questions, go to public meetings and find out who runs your town. These are often the people who need to be influenced to make positive environmental changes in your area. Write to them by name, not just by job title. Let them know that you know who they are.

Use allotments

Allotments, or small pieces of land owned and loaned by local governments, are popular all over the world. They are especially valuable for people who live in high-rise flats without gardens. Share one with a friend for mutual encouragement, though it is advisable not to take on a huge one unless you have had experience. You could grow a substantial part of your fresh food on an allotment. The organic gardener and writer John Jeavons has estimated that it is possible to grow enough fresh food for one year's consumption on a plot just 3 metres (10 feet) square.

Stand for election

If politicians ignore your environmental concerns, get them voted out of office! Local elections are easier to contest than you think, and if you feel particularly inspired, why not get involved with the decision-making process and do it from the top! Before you join a party, carry out a thorough assessment of each party's record on and commitment to the environment.

Go on trails and walks

Find out about your area. Join up with local walking clubs or set off on your own or with the family. Walking can be

pleasurable, relaxing and educational. It doesn't use any energy
other than your own and makes you aware of your surroundings.

Support your local museum

Find out about your local history. It could help you in a case
against bad planning applications, or when trying to save a
particular green area or condemned building. Museums are a
mine of information. They often hold the only records of
your parish, town or city. Ask your museum to consider
keeping local records of ecological changes and even wildlife
sightings. Get nature groups involved.

Save local landmarks

Look at your skyline; it tells a story. The chimneys and church
spires are landmarks of your town. They represent your cultural
heritage and can show the state of your environment at a glance.
Is the landscape full of high-rise flats or factories with pollution
billowing out? Wherever you live, look after important local
landmarks. Get them listed, registered and protected if necessary.

Lobby for safer streets

Women feel especially vulnerable in badly lit streets,
dangerous-looking underpasses and dark walkways set close to
hedgerows and walls. Safer streets can be achieved more
easily than you think. Good planning in favour of women
and low-energy lighting make all the difference. Lobby your
authority about a street near you that could be made safer. It
is part of our environment too.

Support local crafts

Local crafts are part of your heritage and supporting them

benefits the environment. Local jobs are created, diversity is encouraged, transportation reduced and energy saved as local goods fulfil our needs.

Arrange a Sunday walk

People like to walk on a Sunday afternoon so why not take them on an ecological tour? Adopt a theme, such as local churches, canals, a fun walk or interesting buildings. Point out special features and encourage people to take an interest in their area again. This consciousness-raising is an important way to get people to appreciate and respect their local environment.

Record your history

Local residents often have much to say, especially those whose families have been in the area for many generations. Find out what has changed over the years and what has stayed the same, what people like about their area and what worries them; then use modern technology to let the rest of the world know about it.

Hold a green fair

Environment weeks, green fairs and local celebrations bring a community together. Share ideas and resources with like-minded people and join up for a fun time. Get information from ecology organizations, ask charities and voluntary groups to help raise money by organizing bric-à-brac stalls or selling marmalade, for example, and get quizzes, raffles and competitions going. And have fun!

Brighten up your walls

Murals and mosaics brighten up walls in urban areas. In rural areas, walls provide habitats for plants, insects and all manner of animals, including snakes and lizards. Most countryside walls are very old. Built from sandstone, limestone, granite or slate they act as continuous landscape features. Looking after walls is important, especially to maintain a habitat for animals in the face of disappearing hedgerows.

Protect buildings

Buildings can make your community look good or bad, but they have a more important role in the environment. Old churches can house tawny owls or pipistrelle bats. Abandoned houses can be full of mice and bugs. Buildings over a certain age can be protected with special orders, so they cannot be destroyed without good reason. Converting houses and flats creates useful work, saves resources and energy and provides much-needed accommodation. Protect buildings around you and make good use of them.

Don't concrete over everything

Don't allow developers to concrete over everything. Concrete seals in and kills the soil underneath it, making the land no longer productive or pretty. Opt for parks and gardens, playing fields and courtyards of fresh earth, flowers and grass.

Don't be a NIMBY

NIMBYs (Not In My Back Yard) may not want nuclear waste, toxic drums, landfill sites, new factories or blocks of flats in their backyard, but they are quite willing to put it in yours. We all have to take responsibility for the planet. The consequences of our actions cannot be resolved by giving them to someone else. The USA ships its toxic waste to developing countries. Japan ships its nuclear waste to Britain and Britain ships its pesticides to the Philippines. If the company you work for installs a dangerous plant in another town, it is doing the same thing. Don't be a NIMBY. Influence your community.

Ask your local media to get involved

Ask your local radio station, newspaper or even television news to run more features about the environment. What about a regular phone-in with local environmental group organizers on the panel? Or a programme to highlight a local ecological attraction or problem? The media can get through to a lot more people and answer some of their questions easily. Try contacting your local media and asking them.

Adopt a seat

Many local communities benefit from proper seating made of ash or beech. Some have adoption schemes where you can buy a seat with your name on in a park or woodland area for a price that includes its upkeep. This can be especially useful when local authorities cannot afford to maintain seating and let it fall into disrepair.

Take part in public inquiries

Public inquiries exist for you to place on record your concern or support for developments within your community. Some public inquiries last only a few days and planning applications for new buildings or road-building schemes are won or lost very quickly. The application to build a nuclear power station at Hinkley in Somerset found that over 30,000 members of the public objected and many of them gave their objections verbally. It was an important way for the community to say exactly what they felt about the proposal. Enquiries can be successful. Get involved, take part in public inquiries regarding the future of your town.

Swap your specialist knowledge

If you are good at something like gardening, raising finance, baking or sewing, why not swap your knowledge and skills with someone who can offer you something that you need? Skills shares operate in communities around the world very successfully. You could set up a local directory and network.

Set up a local nature reserve

Nature reserves can transform a blighted area into an ecological paradise. Contact your local authority for information about the area of land you have in mind. Set up a local wildlife group and apply for grants and funding to keep the project running. Some local nature reserves have been organized with the cooperation of local schools and some with local community associations. Try to get as many different types of people involved so that everyone can benefit.

Collect stamps and bottle-tops

Collect used stamps and bottle-tops and send them to groups like Oxfam. As well as recycling, you help them to raise funds for sustainable projects overseas.

Local Government

Local politics are often easier to influence than you think. The main problem is cash, but with the right encouragement the environment can be the number-one priority. Find out who your local representative is. Organize yourself to lobby and campaign to get policies like those listed below on the agenda.

Policy

Encourage local participation in environmental initiatives. Support environmental and conservation groups and other non-statutory bodies by providing facilities and space.

Involve local people in decisions on the environment.

Provide clear, simple information to local people about their environment.

Ensure that all committees, staff and departments in local government consider the environmental impact and implications of their activities as routine.

Devise a purchasing policy which bans environmentally damaging products.

Do not buy tropical hardwoods from unsustainable sources for floors, doors and veneers, or for desks and office furniture.

Minimize the use of car-owner requirements in job advertisements. Do not ask for 'owner drivers' in job advertisements unless it is absolutely necessary.

Pollution

Clean up the local area by controlling and reducing litter, particularly by providing regular collections.

Provide free skips to neighbourhoods for householders to get rid of large items with ease.

Stop municipal waste-incineration.

Work with local traders and businesses to provide sponsored litter-bins.

Monitor and regularly check abandoned vehicles.

Stop the transportation of nuclear waste through the area.

Find the most environmentally safe way of disposing of toxic and other non-recyclable waste.

Regularly monitor pollution levels in the streets and provide an information service to members of the public.

Survey and replace all lead pipes still connected to the main water supply.

Enforce local by-laws on noise and noise levels, especially when relating to traffic.

Clean up eyesores that blight local areas.

Introduce a 'hotline' telephone service so that local people can call about pollution worries and problems.

Encourage residents to report waste-dumping and fly-tipping and to respect their local environment.

Clean up graffiti.

Provide rubbish-bins, chutes and bin-stores in council property and on council land.

Clean up any waterways.

Greening

Turn vacant sites over to local nature or conservation groups who can transform them into wildlife havens.

Improve the visual environment of local communities by creating grassed and wildlife areas, providing for better fencing and gardens and painting and cleaning up buildings.

Register and promote the use of allotments for local people and create new allotment areas.

Encourage wild species of flora and fauna whenever possible.

Encourage local businesses to open up land owned by them for public use or for wildlife.

Carry out a wildlife survey with local ecology and conservation groups.

Encourage window-boxes, tree and shrub planting and more wild flowers on council-owned property.

Provide park and street furniture that is sympathetic to the local environment, but not from tropical hardwood sources.

Agree to minimize the impact of new development plans on local habitats and wildlife areas, taking special consideration of trees.

Encourage the growth of woodland areas, especially the planting of local species.

Encourage new wildlife and nature walks within the area.

Improve the facilities offered for recreation and play, to enhance the environment and to improve opportunities.

Transport

Improve road-safety measures, including 'traffic-calming' schemes, bollards and facilities for handicapped or elderly people, such as non-slip surfaces.

Repair roads, signposts and potholes.

Provide adequate cycle-lane facilities and secure parking in all public places.

Restrict car-parking in central areas and restrict lorries in specified areas.

Promote public transport by subsidizing fares for the unemployed and disadvantaged. Provide subsidized transport services for women, especially at night.

Always consider improving public transport systems rather than building new roads.

Ensure all vehicles owned by officials run on unleaded petrol and phase in the use of transport with catalytic converters.

Reassess the use of official vehicles and where appropriate find other means of transport.

Consider providing company bicycles.

Housing

Improve security on local government property with better lighting and security locks.

Ensure that all new building developments are well designed, improve the area and are sympathetic to surrounding buildings.

Provide design guides for local businesses and home-owners on shop-fronting, dry maintenance, roofing, windows, energy conservation and so on.

Create a scientific information team to monitor and assess pollution-related issues within the area.

Provide testing facilities for the chemical analysis of air, water, soil and food.

Scientific advice

Replace all CFC or halon products in use and provide disposal facilities for the public.

Monitor the safety of ground water and take appropriate steps to prosecute local businesses and water authorities that fall foul of regulations on water quality.

Arrange facilities to warn local residents of levels of radiation.

Arrange for swimming pools to phase out the use of chlorine as a disinfectant and opt for ozone (O_3) as an alternative.

Restrict the use of pesticides wherever possible.

Provide strict safety guidelines for workers using pesticides.

Introduce pesticide-free zones in public recreation areas.

Introduce codes for local building sites, including agreements on noise levels, pollution and dust control.

Oppose new incineration plants. Work to remove chlorine sources from hospital incinerators and crematoria. Stop municipal incineration, and call for the closure of toxic-waste incinerators.

Offer dog-training classes.

Ensure that there are sufficient by-laws to regulate dog fouling.

The reusable is mightier than the disposable.

Recycling

Ensure that the local authority has sufficient recycling facilities for all materials, including hazardous household waste.

Develop a recycling policy which reduces the amount of waste produced so that less waste has to be collected. Educate the public about reusing as much waste as possible and recycle all available materials

Use unbleached, recycled paper for internal and external communications.

Whenever possible, encourage the use of recycling facilities at local supermarket car parks.

Encourage local stores to promote minimal, recyclable packaging.

Provide a wood-salvaging centre to encourage the public to bring, buy and reuse timber.

Ensure that as much timber as possible is saved for recycling during rehabilitation or demolition of council-owned property.

Ban the use of tropical hardwoods obtained from non-sustainable sources.

Energy

Offer the public general, technical and scientific information and support on energy conservation measures.

Provide maximum energy efficiency in all authority buildings.

Investigate combined heat-and-power programmes for local council buildings.

Carry out energy audits on estates, educational facilities and managed properties.

Insulate offices and managed property.

Use passive solar energy conservation when designing or planning new buildings.

Health and animal welfare

Offer organic vegetables and vegetarian food in council canteens and encourage staff to eat a healthier diet.

Adopt a fox code; foxes are not dangerous in any area, even urban foxes. Stop the persecution, hunting and gassing of this highly intelligent creature.

Always use non-animal-tested products in preference to those tested on animals.

Discourage local shops from selling furs, ivory and other products from endangered species.

Build a centre for ecological studies as part of council educational and recreational facilities.

Undertake not to purchase known cancer-causing substances.

National Government

Many of the things that have to be done to safeguard our environment cannot be done without commitment from, and action by, politicians and government officials. They must be lobbied, written to and visited so that they make the environment priority locally, nationally and internationally. Below is a list of some of the important policies which should be carried out by environmentally conscious politicians. Ask your politician what he or she is doing.

Defence

Our governments spend millions on defending us, with increasing amounts being spent on high-technology warfare at the cost of some of our civil-defence plans. In the ecological crisis much of the scientific expertise will be wasted unless we begin now to reallocate tasks and money into protection of our environment rather than aggression against other countries. Here is a tiny sample of some of the things governments can do to reallocate resources to save the planet.

Re-equip NATO and Warsaw Pact engineering units for disaster relief and protection from global warming emergencies.

Convert nuclear submarines and high-flying military aircraft for long-term oceanic and atmospheric monitoring.

Change the use of our satellite monitoring systems to target key areas suffering from environmental degradation problems, such as deforestation.

Pollution

Pollution from the land, sea and air is poisoning our food, our water and our bodies. The British Government recorded levels of dioxins 100 times higher than their safety guidelines in mothers' breast-milk samples during 1989. Lung and heart charities issued warnings for people in cities like London and Toronto about the build-up of photochemical smog. The air we breathe and the water we drink is central to our survival and it should be any government's top priority to ensure that it is safe and clean.

The pollution that we see around us is having an even more serious effect on wildlife and on our flora and fauna. Thousands of dead seals have been washed ashore in the last few years because of a mystery virus. The pollution contamination has reached sea mammals, the top of the aquatic food chain; and we are next. The measures listed below are just some of the things that governments can do to ensure that we have a future.

Implement fully the Control of Pollution Act.

Set up collection points for hazardous waste in every town.

Establish strict safety procedures for handling chemicals.

Ban any form of industrial dumping in seas, rivers and oceans, including dumping from the shore.

Halt any further expansion of the incineration programme and phase out those plants already operating.

Restrict the production of packaging that is not made with environmentally sound and recyclable material.

Clean up beaches and extend the January 1989 Regulations, on the dumping of plastics at sea, to cover dumping of plastics from coastal areas, including from sewers.

Ban the import of chlorine-bleached paper and pulp derivatives like rayon that use chlorine.

Prosecute and fine heavily companies that pollute the environment.

Ban all CFC and halon products and provide more finance for research into alternatives.

Enforce international agreements protecting small cetaceans from pollution, overfishing, habitat destruction and tuna fishing.

Require commercial and industrial producers of waste to be licensed.

Set up enforcement teams to stop the illegal dumping of toxic waste at sea and bring those companies and individuals involved to justice.

Stop the dumping of untreated sewage into the oceans and seas and research new ways of using sewage as manure.

Monitor and prosecute companies that risk the lives of local inhabitants through pollution and industrial waste from factories.

Energy

The greenhouse effect can be halted with a sensible energy policy. A government's policy should be concentrated on using as little energy as possible for the maximum return, instead of the current thinking which simply allows energy to be used with no regard for environmental concerns. Energy conservation is the first step. Money and resources also have to be put into researching renewable sources of energy for the future. The following recommendations represent some of the more important steps to take.

Decommission existing nuclear power stations.

Halt further work on the Fast Breeder Reactor Programme.

Limit radioactive and polluting emissions from nuclear power stations.

End radioactive discharges into the Irish Sea from Sellafield and stop reprocessing.

Agree on-site storage of nuclear waste.

Reallocate staff from nuclear power stations to research renewable energy and nuclear waste management and disposal.

Increase grants to small businesses and individuals for energy conservation measures.

Where necessary, subsidize, lend or give grants to people receiving public welfare so that they can buy energy efficient equipment, such as low-energy light-bulbs, efficient cookers, fridges, boilers, insulation and so on.

Enact a national Energy Efficiency Act requiring companies and contractors to produce goods and build houses with high mandatory efficiency standards.

Global concerns

Global co-operation is crucial for our survival. Now more than ever we have realized that environmental pollution recognizes no political boundaries. Crucial to the fight to save our planet is the co-operation and help that we give to the Third World countries. For so long we have used their people and land as a cheap source of labour and food that we have helped to destroy millions of acres of once productive land. Our help to them should be empowering, not tying them to a series of stringent, Western policy prescriptions, including mounting debt. Nor can we continue to use the Third World as a toxic waste-bin for our industries, just because the waste is too dangerous to be dealt with on our own territory.

Ban the cross-border shipment of any toxic or hazardous waste.

Offer scientific, financial and political support to Third World countries who wish to ban the cross-border shipment of any toxic or hazardous waste.

Support only development projects that are environmentally sustainable and take account of the needs of women.

Legislate to ensure that hardwood imports from the tropics for industry come only from sustainable sources.

Press for relief for the poorest countries on debts owed to the World Bank and International Monetary Fund and for some debts to be cancelled completely.

Increase the amount of government money spent on aid to developing countries to bring us into line with the rest of Europe and the United Nations. The target is at least 0.7 per cent of the Gross National Product.

Sign an international treaty to recognize Antarctica as an independent continent and help to protect it as a national park.

Use all space programme facilities to research and devise new means to protect the atmosphere of the earth, especially the ozone layer.

Ban all NASA, Ariane and Soyuz rockets, shuttles and boosters which use freon gases and eject chlorine-containing compounds that destroy the ozone layer.

Transport

The bias in government transport policy in favour of the car must be ended. The car has become one of the world's largest polluters, producing the chemicals that cause the greenhouse effect, acid rain and damage to human beings through lead and other pollutants. An understanding of the harm caused by cars must inform any new transport policy and a new approach would have to recognize that new roads, motorways and cars will never solve the problems of transporting people from home to work and back again. The recommendations below are a selection of those that could start to see a regeneration of services, now almost in crisis because of current policy.

Reallocate road expenditure to provide better facilities for pedestrians and cyclists.

Phase out leaded petrol.

Phase out two-star petrol.

Research the impact of, and produce recommendations and legislation to cover, the environmental effect of diesel oils in transport.

Halt all further motorway and road plans and agree specific environmental criteria for new transport developments.

Phase out the manufacture and sale of cars without catalytic converters.

Charge drivers who use cars in cities such as London and Manchester.

Remove any further subsidies on company cars.

Lower speed limits to encourage road safety and the efficient use of fuel resources.

Subsidize rail and bus networks to the same levels as the rest of the EEC and encourage the public to use them as widely as possible through cheaper fares and better services.

Investigate other forms of transportation including river systems, light railways and trams.

Agriculture and countryside

Farm land is suffering, small farmers continue to go out of business and the condition of our soil is becoming progressively poor due to intensive methods which are stripping the soil of its nutrients. Over 44 per cent of British soil is at risk from soil erosion; the European Parliament recorded that over 2 million hectares (5 million acres) were threatened in Britain. Even so, organic farming is largely ignored by the British Government, and current policies do not encourage sustainable farming methods. There are many things that farmers, ecologists and even international leaders have suggested should be done to save and protect the future of our countryside. A holistic approach is now long overdue and many fear that unless intense pressure is brought to bear on Parliament there may be no time left for debate.

Improve the quality of drinking water, including, if necessary, bringing the water authorities back into public ownership.

Restrict the use of nitrogen fertilizers, and observe the World Health Organization's recommended limit of 50 milligrams of nitrate in each litre (1.7 pints) of drinking water.

Greatly increase research into non-chemical pest control.

Offer subsidies to farmers to encourage them to switch to organic farming.

Ban battery barn, semi-intensive, litter and perchery methods of keeping chickens.

Ban growth hormones and stimulants in animals for the food industry.

End subsidies to farmers to graze protected moorlands or wetlands.

Ban the ritual slaughter of any animal.

Ban the import of inhumanely reared veal.

Encourage mixed farming.

Halt all drainage grants which destroy valuable wetlands, and protect those wetland areas remaining.

Abolish export subsidies for food so that excess production can be sold on the world market without subsidy.

Label all food products clearly with specific percentages of ingredients and details of the pesticides used in their production.

Label all consumer goods such as cleaning materials with their contents.

Develop agricultural policies that give priority to the needs of developing countries before ours, including halting the practice of dumping foodstuffs on the market which destroys the market in those countries.

Provide funds for and carry out proper protection of all sites of special scientific interest and environmentally sensitive areas.

Ban all forms of destructive forestry subsidized through tax concessions.

Legislate for planning controls for farming and forestry operations, where they affect hedges, trees and woodlands and the conversion of land to other uses.

Ban the use of chemicals on land that has never been treated with pesticides or herbicides, such as ancient woodlands and meadows.

Protect and increase the numbers of national nature reserves and national parks.

Grants and payments for the planting of broad-leaved trees should be increased and planting of non-native species should be phased out.

The results of pesticide toxicity tests carried out by industry should be published and made freely available to the public.

Animal protection

Animals have been cruelly treated by big business and the argument that they do not suffer or feel pain is no longer tenable. We must find a way of supporting our species on this planet without the continuous torture and inhumane practices that have been the norm in the last fifty years. Governments can provide the means for legislation to put a stop to some of the worst practices. These are just some of the protection measures that governments can take.

Ban the LD50 animal test which determines the single lethal dose of a chemical on animals on the basis that 50 per cent of the animals die.

Replace animal experiments by devising and funding humane research programmes using a variety of alternative methods.

Implement the 117 recommendations for improvements in British slaughterhouses recommended by the Farm Animal Welfare Council.

Reintroduce dog licences and make the fee payable to local authorities so that they can fund dog warden schemes.

Provide extra funding for charities and research bodies to find alternatives to using animals in cancer research.

Enforce the British 1975 ban on smoking experiments using dogs.

Require companies to stop the use of animals for testing food, toiletry and other products.

Provide legislation to enable monitoring and protection of animals such as foxes in urban areas and amphibians, birds and butterflies in green areas around the country.

Policy

Government policy needs to change fast. Representatives who put profit before survival need to re-examine their priorities. But policy changes that make any difference have to come from the top and the only people who can change the ideas of those at the top is the public. Letters and lobbying on specific issues raises concern but fundamental changes must be linked to a change of priorities from the public. Let politicians know how you think the planet should be saved.

Provide a requirement for environmental-impact assessments

for each new project, building or decision by national government.

Incorporate environmental matters into the policy of every government department and its ministers.

Set up an Environmental Protection Agency in the UK to combine research and policy on a wide range of environmental problems.

Provide resources and new funding for economic developments which make good use of local resources and provide for local needs.

Increase the numbers of jobs in conservation work and in scientific research on ecology and environmentalism.

Fund the development and restoration of buildings for new housing, community buildings and other uses.

Ensure that government tenders list environmental criteria as a concern. They should include assessments of how new projects may affect the environment.

Encourage less consumption.

A Freedom of Information Charter is needed to let the public know about potential and actual hazards and their effects.

Civil Liberties

Invest and shop for the advancement of women

Women make up 52 per cent of the human population of the world. They do most of the world's work, but they own less than 1 per cent of the world's land. The lives of women in Third World countries have become much harder over the last twenty years, for a variety of reasons. In most countries women are not seen as men's equals. Yet at the same time they are expected to produce and care for the next generation. Women can contribute greatly to saving the planet and should be encouraged wherever possible. Invest in women-owned business and support women's cooperatives, positive schemes to aid equal opportunities and the Women's Environmental Network.

Stop multinationals exploiting women in developing countries

Bottle-feeding is a major cause of child diarrhoea and 200,000 deaths are recorded annually in Pakistan alone. Producers of breast-milk substitutes have been issued with an international code for marketing and selling their product in developing countries. But reports from the Philippines, Pakistan and Malaysia tell of violations at every possible level. Malaysian groups report wholesale blackmail by companies that give the formula free in maternity hospitals, telling women that because westerners drink it, it is the best food for their baby.

This costs mothers much of their badly needed income when a free and safe alternative, breast-milk, is available.

End double standards

One multinational sells the pesticide dieldrin (banned on British-grown potatoes) to the Philippines for use on exotic fruits which are then exported back to Britain. Workers are poorly advised about the health risks from using such chemicals, thought too dangerous for our consumption. No food, chemical, technology, pesticide or experiment which has been banned in western countries should be dumped on the developing world. Our high standards should be applied globally. Multinationals should have a duty to be responsible to the world, not just to their shareholders.

Help the homeless and hungry

Homelessness is not just a feature of the starving in Africa. There are over 250,000 homeless families in the UK, twice as many as ten years ago. Often families end up in cheap bed-and-breakfast hotels without cooking facilities or privacy. Their environment and their bad diet mean that they face a serious health risk, young children and babies especially.

Support tribal peoples

Tribal people living in rainforest areas across the world are in danger. They have lived in and protected the forest for centuries, living in balance and harmony. Today our form of 'development' is destroying them. Whole communities are being wiped out by western diseases such as measles and chicken-pox, illnesses unheard of before we came along. Children are dying of lung diseases because of the dust caused by building new roads through the forest. These people know the plants and fruits of the forest intimately – that is why they have survived for so long. They have given us many of our new medicines and foods. We have no right to impose our lifestyle and diseases on these people. Support groups that work to save the tribal people's rights and dignity.

Campaign for disabled access

Our transport system is dominated by roads, which are built for able-bodied car drivers. Pedestrians and cyclists take second place. Only 40 per cent of British women hold current driving licences, the remainder having to rely on public transport and walking. The section of our society that really suffers from bad access, however, is disabled people. Potholes, lack of safe places to cross, high kerbs and tiny pavements are all hazards. But think about trying to get on a bus or tube with a wheelchair. Virtually impossible as well as dangerous. Have we got the right to confine people to their homes because we will not accommodate them on the streets or on public transport?

Reclaim your right to walk

In Britain it is an offence for a motorist not to give you priority at a zebra crossing, but many motorists forget because they are so much faster and feel superior to mere pedestrians. You have as much right to be walking on the road as they have to drive, and you do not cause pollution, accidents and hazards, or waste energy. 'Traffic-calming' schemes, car-free areas and pedestrian precincts all help in urban areas. The Ramblers Association promotes the protection of rights for the walker in the countryside and has campaigned for access to open country since 1935. We still have a long way to go.

Stand up for children's rights

Some 75 million children worldwide under the age of 15 are forced to work for a living. They have to help to pay off their family debts, because of the costs of modernization in agriculture, the destruction of local habitats and forests, including rainforests, and the increasing burden of debt placed on farmers by the world's large banks and financial institutions. An international code of human rights includes rights for children. This should be supported around the world.

Take direct action

Direct action is not confined solely to Greenpeace activists in boats, throwing themselves in front of nuclear warships. It is something we can all do and it is easier than you think. Why not begin by telling someone in the street not to drop litter if you see them? Or by sending back a chemical product to the manufacturer asking them to dispose of it carefully? Or by handing out leaflets outside your hardwood store, which sells wood from rainforests? Or even by deciding to stand up yourself for the things you believe in, by boycotting products from companies that could destroy your environment? Stand up for yourself and the planet!

Fight for compensation for victims of environmental disasters

The Bhopal disaster in 1984 affected over 600,000 people, most of whom have still not received help financially, or even medically. Only 120,000 claimants have been assessed for government help so far. The company concerned, Union Carbide, has offered a final settlement of £294 million ($470 million), but money is not the only problem. It will not bring back the 3,150 who died. Medical care is needed by 500,000 victims. The leak of toxic methyl isocyanate gas raises serious questions about the propriety of companies producing such dangerous poisons so close to where people live. Highly dangerous isocyanates are used in the manufacture of resins, specialist paints and sealants. If we cut down on our use of these chemicals we can cut down on the chances of another accident.

Invest and shop for the right to know

We all need information and facts to form opinions about the environment, development, politics and our lives in general. Companies are usually not required by law to offer us information and facts about their operations and yet we give them billions of pounds. Ask companies to list ingredients, give accounts and research results more freely so that we can make up our own minds. Support those companies that give information. Your investment in their future could stop other companies that are less open.

Don't buy cash crops

Cash crops are commodities from developing countries, such as cocoa, coffee, tea and peanuts. We have engineered a system of production which means that developing countries stop growing food for themselves and start growing exotic or specialist foods for us, the richer nations. This uses up land, pesticides and severely imbalances the local ecosystem. During the worst years of the Ethiopian famine, when pictures of dead children were broadcast all over the world, the Ethiopian people had a bumper crop of peanuts but could not eat a single one. They all had to be shipped to the north to pay off crippling debts imposed by us in the first place. Only world condemnation of this sort of contradiction will stop the vicious circle of poverty for the majority of the planet's population. A dramatic curtailing of our desire for too great a variety of specialist foods will also make a difference.

Give equal consideration to animals

Pain is pain. Non-human animals experience pain. As human animals we consider ourselves superior to non-humans and inflict pain of all kinds on animals to maintain our lifestyles (as in medical research and cosmetic testing), or even for pure pleasure (as in hunting and animal sports). Non-human animals cannot speak our language, but consideration of feelings must be the basis on which we begin to respect the non-human animal world. Animals feel pain and suffer if hit, drugged, deprived of food, light or water, and it is time we woke up to that. Our species' superiority is not a justification. We would not consider maltreating a six-month-old baby just because it could not speak, vote, fight back or in-tellectualize, so why should we do it to an animal?

Support disarmament

Trillions of dollars are spent worldwide on weapons of war that we hope we will never use, while much-needed cash that could be used to feed the hungry and protect the environment is missing. Global concern is now shifting from arms to the environment, but as yet the resources being spent on the former are not being reallocated to save the latter. Only a massive change of heart by governments across the world will stop us wasting precious resources on arms to kill. Redirect military funds towards sustainable development.

Learn the law

There are many laws affecting the environment, some of them international. The International Maritime Organization, for example, has jurisdiction on the sea and oceans, while the United Nations can issue rulings on the rights of people. Governments legislate for companies operating within their own boundaries, but they often cannot control their activities outside those boundaries. Learn the laws affecting environmental and human degradation. Without knowing what they are you will not be able to exert any influence.

Campaign for the right of common access

We need the right to walk freely in our countryside. Free access does not mean that we have the right to damage crops or walls, buildings or fences. Ramblers and walkers should avoid walking over gardens and areas where crops grow, but farmers in turn should not plough up paths for crops and should avoid the practice of putting barbed wire up to prevent access. The right of common access for those on foot should be a central part of our future countryside policy.

Commit yourself

Commit yourself to an ecological lifestyle: recycle waste, eat good food, repair and reuse, buy additive-free and chemical-free, think small, walk and cycle, be aware of local initiatives, avoid exploitation and use your power as a consumer whenever possible.

Talk about it

If you have read through over 1,000 ways to save the planet, you will know that you can make a difference and that you are part of the problem as well as part of the solution. Others need to know this too. So here's the last suggestion. Talk to them, read more about the subject, do something positive. Join the millions who are already trying to save our planet.

Useful Addresses

Many non-profit groups work on a shoestring. If you're writing to them, please enclose a stamped addressed envelope and give them a clear idea of what you want.

Animal Aid
7 Castle Street, Tonbridge, Kent, TN9 1BH

Ark
500 Harrow Road, London W9 3QA

Auro non-toxic DIY products
Saffron Walden 0799 24744

British Union for the Abolition of Vivisection
16a Crane Grove, London, N7 8LB

Campaign for Nuclear Disarmament
22–24 Underwood Street, London, N1 7JQ

Centre for Alternative Technology
Machynlleth, Powys, SY20 9AZ

Common Ground
45 Shelton Street, London, WC2H 9HJ

Council for Acupuncture
Suite 1, 19a Cavendish Square, London, W1M 9AD

The Countryside Commission
John Dower House, Crescent Place, Cheltenham,
Gloucestershire, GL50 3RA

Deep Ecology Workshops/Council of All Beings
Helen Sieroda, 56 Ashley Road, London, N19 3AF

Henry Doubleday Research Association
Ryton-on-Dunsmore, Coventry West Midlands CV8 3LG

Environmental Investigations Agency
208–209 Upper Street, London, N1 1RL

The Ethical Investment Research and Information Service
401 Bondway Business Centre, 71 Bondway, London,
SW8 1SQ

Friends of the Earth
26 Underwood Street, London, N1 7JQ

The Green Party
10 Station Parade, Balham High Road, London, SW12 9AZ

Greenpeace
30–31 Islington Green, London, N1 8BR

House of Commons
London, SW1A 0AA

London Hazards Centre
3rd Floor, Headland House, 308 Gray's Inn Road, London,
WC1X 8DS

Mailing Preference Service (to get your name off unsolicited
mailings)
Freepost 22, London, W1E 7EZ

The Nature Conservancy Council
Northminster House, Peterborough PE1 1UA

Neighbourhood Energy Action
2–4 Bigg Market, Newcastle upon Tyne, NE1 1VW

Oxfam
Oxfam House, 274 Banbury Road, Oxford, OX2 7DZ

The Pesticides Trust
20 Compton Terrace, London, N1 2UN

Ramblers Association
1–5 Wandsworth Road, London, SW8 2XX

Royal Society for the Prevention of Cruelty to Animals
The Causeway, Horsham, West Sussex, RH12 1HG

Royal Society for the Protection of Birds
The Lodge, Sandy, Bedfordshire, SE1 2DL

The Seed Bank and Exchange
Cowcombe Farm, Gipsy Lane, Chalford, Stroud,
Gloucestershire, GL6 8HP

The Society of Homoeopaths
2 Artizan Road, Northampton, NN1 4HU

Soil Association
86 Colston Street, Bristol, BS1 5BB

Survival International
310 Edgware Road, London, W2 1DY

Traidcraft
Kingsway, Gateshead, Tyne & Wear, NE11 0NE

Vegetarian Society
Parkdale, Dunham Road, Altrincham, Cheshire, WA14 4QG

Whale and Dolphin Conservation Society
20 West Lea Road, Bath, Avon, BA1 3RL

Women's Environmental Network
287 City Road, London, EC1V 1LA

Working Weekends on Organic Farms
19 Bradford Road, Lewes, Sussex, BN7 1RB

World Wildlife Fund
Panda House, Weyside Park, Catteshall Lane, Godalming,
Surrey GU7 1XR

FOR THE BEST IN PAPERBACKS, LOOK FOR THE 🐧

In every corner of the world, on every subject under the sun, Penguin represents quality and variety – the very best in publishing today.

For complete information about books available from Penguin – including Puffins, Penguin Classics and Arkana – and how to order them, write to us at the appropriate address below. Please note that for copyright reasons the selection of books varies from country to country.

In the United Kingdom: Please write to *Dept E.P., Penguin Books Ltd, Harmondsworth, Middlesex, UB7 0DA.*

If you have any difficulty in obtaining a title, please send your order with the correct money, plus ten per cent for postage and packaging, to *PO Box No 11, West Drayton, Middlesex*

In the United States: Please write to *Dept BA, Penguin, 299 Murray Hill Parkway, East Rutherford, New Jersey 07073*

In Canada: Please write to *Penguin Books Canada Ltd, 2801 John Street, Markham, Ontario L3R 1B4*

In Australia: Please write to the *Marketing Department, Penguin Books Australia Ltd, P.O. Box 257, Ringwood, Victoria 3134*

In New Zealand: Please write to the *Marketing Department, Penguin Books (NZ) Ltd, Private Bag, Takapuna, Auckland 9*

In India: Please write to *Penguin Overseas Ltd, 706 Eros Apartments, 56 Nehru Place, New Delhi, 110019*

In the Netherlands: Please write to *Penguin Books Nederland B.V., Postbus 195, NL–1380AD Weesp*

In West Germany: Please write to *Penguin Books Ltd, Friedrichstrasse 10–12, D–6000 Frankfurt/Main 1*

In Spain: Please write to *Longman Penguin España, Calle San Nicolas 15, E–28013 Madrid*

In Italy: Please write to *Penguin Italia s.r.l., Via Como 4, I-20096 Pioltello (Milano)*

In France: Please write to *Penguin Books Ltd, 39 Rue de Montmorency, F-75003 Paris*

In Japan: Please write to *Longman Penguin Japan Co Ltd, Yamaguchi Building, 2–12–9 Kanda Jimbocho, Chiyoda-Ku, Tokyo 101*